I0407539

About The Authors

Dr. James R. Fury and Dr. Lawrence A. Watson are Clinical Psychologists. They have been treating patients of all ages and for a variety of psychological, emotional, and behavioral difficulties for nearly 60 years combined. They have treated patients for a wide range of diagnoses including depression, bipolar disorder, obsessive compulsive disorder, generalized anxiety disorder, panic disorder, and perhaps the Grand Mammy of them all, borderline personality disorder.

Through their work, and as colleagues who communicate together on a regular basis, they began to discuss seeing patterns of behavioral and psychological disturbances that seemed to share common threads, no matter what the official diagnosis was, or official reasons for seeking treatment. These common "threads" were not unique at all, and were seen as quite ubiquitous in nature, for some individuals, but not for others Eventually, in a discussion designed to be part of peer supervision, the practice of running difficult cases by a trusted colleague or colleagues, they both almost simultaneously stated the obvious out loud. That the common threads of disturbance seen in many of their patients, and in their spouses, family members, etc. were astoundingly confined to gender lines! That these problems, so severe, and so difficult to both treat as professionals, or to deal with in personal relationships, were inextricably confined to females and females alone! The fact that this seemed obvious on one level, yet never previously discussed frankly and openly, in the true manner in which it exists, begged Dr. Watson and Dr. Fury to communicate what they had come to know, to the world. And thus, AWAP was born.

AWAP

Yes, that's right! All women are psychotic. Ok, not exactly. By psychotic I am talking about all women being borderline. "Borderline" or Borderline personality disorder, as it now referred to currently, is a personality disorder, or a set or behavioral and emotional traits and tendencies, that were originally thought of as being "almost psychotic" or "borderline psychotic", hence the term borderline. The condition is characterized by a pattern of highly unstable and sometimes dangerous behavior, mood swings, etc. that we will soon describe in greater detail. What we will now begin to demonstrate, is that all women possess the "seeds" to develop these tendencies, and are at-risk for developing the full blown syndrome or disorder. How can this be? How can all women have the underpinnings of what is considered to be a quite severe psychological or psychiatric disorder? Well, as shocking and controversial as this thesis may be, we will carefully and fully lay out our case.

As stated in our preface, after decades of clinical practice and personal experience, we began to connect the dots and realized that without question, all females indeed suffer from the disturbances of having borderline personalities. It may not really surprise you, but girls and women account for the majority of psychotherapy patients. That is a fact. Females are nearly twice as likely to seek out treatment than are males. There are a number of reasons for this, including psychosocial factors, cultural factors, and the reason that is most relevant here: They have issues! All right, males have issues also. We all know that. Males are far more aggressive than females, far more likely to engage in criminal behavior, etc. The fact is the issues are very different in most cases. The "issues' faced by males are much more typically "externalizing" issues. That means they have problems with acting out. Aggression, hyperactivity, criminality. Females tend to have issues that are in some ways, very opposite. They have "internalizing" issues. These include depression, anxiety, parasuicidal behavior (e.g. "cutting"). This is not to say males cannot experience depression and anxiety, etc. Of course they can. But when they do, these disorders typically manifest themselves very differently than in women. "Cutting", or self-mutilation, or self-harm occurs almost exclusively in females. They internalize their issues, and take it out on themselves, because at their core is a deep sense of self-loathing. This, as I will discuss later, can usually be traced to some type of abuse, i.e. verbal, physical, or sexual. It is a fact, that nearly 50% of women report having experienced some type of degrading physical or sexual abuse in their lifetimes.

In addition to the clinical experience, training, and expertise I and Dr. Watson have had, we are human. We have had relationships. We began over the years to detect the common threads that the women in our lives shared with the patients we have treated, which lead us to the inescapable conclusion that all women share at least the potential to become borderline, although most women we have ever encountered exhibit many or most of the most classic signs of the disorder. Perhaps, to a lesser degree than the clinical population, but it is pretty much all there. We will discuss the disorder in both it's extreme forms, which often necessitates intense treatment, and even inpatient treatment and hospitalizations, and the common threads that can be seen in all women, all over the world. We will focus on the manifestation in our modern, western society, and look forward to discussing cross cultural manifestation s in our future work.

Movie fans are familiar with Glen Close's Oscar nominated performance in "Fatal Attraction"(Paramount Pictures, 1987). Her excellent portrayal of the bunny boiler is what we are talking about here in it's most severe and pronounced form, to the point of violence and homicidal rage, but in lesser forms, many of the same characteristics can easily be found by more closely looking, at the "fairer sex", in other words, all females. Let's take a look at the official, clinical formulation. The "disorder", is included in the DSM. The DSM is the official diagnostic "Bible" of the American Psychiatric Association. Here is the section on the diagnosis of Borderline Personality Disorder:

The Diagnostic and Statistical Manual of Mental Disorders-Fifth Edition (DSM-5), defines BPD as such:

To meet a diagnosis of Borderline Personality Disorder under the DSM-V, you must show "a pervasive pattern of instability of interpersonal relationships, self-image, and affects, and marked impulsivity, beginning in early adulthood and present in a variety of contexts, as indicated by five (or more) of the following":

1. *Frantic efforts to avoid real or imagined abandonment*
2. *A pattern of unstable and intense interpersonal relationships characterized by alternating between extremes of idealization and devaluation*
3. *Identity disturbance: markedly and persistently unstable self-image or sense of self*
4. *Impulsivity in at least two areas that are potentially self-damaging (e.g., **substance abuse**, binge eating, and reckless driving)*

5. *Recurrent suicidal behavior, gestures, or threats, or self-mutilating behavior*
6. *Affective instability due to a marked reactivity of mood (e.g., intense episodic dysphoria, irritability, or*

anxiety usually lasting a few hours and only rarely more than a few days)
7. *Chronic feelings of emptiness*
8. *Inappropriate, intense anger or difficulty __controlling anger__ (e.g., frequent displays of temper, constant anger, recurrent physical fights)*
9. *Transient, stress-related paranoid ideation or severe dissociative symptoms*

Now let's explore these symptoms in an objective way. How does one define a pervasive pattern of unstable interpersonal relationships? Perhaps it is creating unnecessary conflict in sexual relationships, friendships, and familial relations. How many times have you or a female loved one said I can't stand that person! Whether it be a parent, sibling, spouse, friend, lover, or even child? This intensity is much more common in females than males. It is often attributed to hormonal imbalance and pre-menstrual syndrome. The unpleasant truth is these relationship patterns are **pervasive** and thus not due to menstrual cycles or menopause.

On the other end of the instability is over-idealization of the targeted person in the relationship. "You are GREATEST guy on the planet! You're smart, sexy, sensitive, caring, and oh so funny!" When hearing this, men, alarm bells should be going off in your head. She may speak of your sexual prowess and tell you how, unmatched you are to all the men in her past. Beware! This will be flattering and ego boosting, until what is called splitting occurs. As amazing as you have been described and as adored as you may be now; the hatred and vehemence is just around the corner. It is important to recognize that all women have some degree of BPD. It may not be as dramatic for some, and the devaluation may be covertly expressed, but it is there. Your wife or girlfriend while only being distant and cold during these periods of time is likely telling her friends and family what a worthless piece of garbage you are. In fact, in my practice I often hear I wish he were dead!

Let's now explore frantic efforts to avoid real or imagined abandonment. Texts, emails, phone messages, social media stalking, physical stalking when a woman is insecure in a relationship are all too common. These behaviors have an addictive quality. I often hear women say, I know it's ridiculous, but I can't stop myself. Often women tolerate extremely unhealthy and abusive relationships, strictly due to this horrific fear of abandonment. Have you ever started dated someone, and they become very angry, because you went a day, or even hours without the phone call or the text? You find yourself surprised by the intensity of the angry reaction. Your reply of, "I was busy", is not going to cut it. The young lady is basically having a mini-form of the splitting reaction. You were great, but now, you are horrible and selfish. You should have called, but you didn't. You didn't even think of it. You have committed your first act of abandonment in this new relationship. Unfortunately, you are bound to commit this over and over again. If you are lucky, a woman will see this initial transgression as a "deal breaker". Especially if the woman is attractive and has many suitors, you may be seen as unfit, and because you are horrible and selfish, and because you will be seen as likely to do this over and over, she may decide that she will never speak to you again!

As for the fragile self-image underpinning borderlineism, this can be found in all aspects of modern culture for women. Cosmetic surgery and Botox treatment, hair straightening, curling and dying, manicures, pedicures, waxing, lasers, obsessive shopping for uncomfortable shoes that alter height, cosmetics, covering oneself in mud, and other substances, skin bleaching, chemical peels, diet pills, and eating disorders all speak to the universality of this disturbed self-image. Women are continuously comparing themselves to other women and specifically, unrealistic ideals of what a woman should look like. When a woman puts on an outfit and asks, "Does this make me look fat?", what is she really saying? This is a symptom of poor self-image, self-loathing, and excessive need for reassurance. If given an honest response such as, "No, the clothes don't make you look fat. It's the chocolate cake you ate last night that makes you look fat.", or even "I find curvy women attractive" a borderline rage will likely ensue.

Impulsive behavior such as binge eating, alcohol and drug abuse, shopping sprees, and sexual acting out behavior are often triggered by "hurt feelings". These hurt feelings are generally a direct reflection of perceived rejection, abandonment, or even an irrational thought regarding people harboring negative feelings about them. Once engaged in the self-destructive behavior, a downward spiral begins. Now the self-loathing for engaging in binge eating, clothes shopping, etc. leads to more negative self-evaluation. Imagine binge eating, excessive spending on clothing that doesn't fit well, painful surgeries, starving, colon cleansing, loss of valuable time and money for the sake of becoming physically acceptable to oneself and others. Because the woman has an unstable body image, none of these extreme measures result in self-acceptance. Now, the resulting emotional reaction often leads to the next topic of self-mutilation, suicidal behaviors, gestures and threats.

Threats of self-injury and suicide are common among women. Successful suicide occurs in both sexes. It is extremely telling that males commit more suicides than women, but women make far more failed suicide attempts. These repeated failed suicides are referred to as suicidal gestures, or parasuicidal behavior. Along with these bogus, attention-seeking suicide attempts women are more likely to engage in self-mutilative behavior than men.

Cutting is the most common form of self-mutilation. These cuts are most often superficial cuts on the arms and/or legs that are easily visible to others. It is described by people with BPD as a relief from all their pain. It goes along with frantic efforts to avoid abandonment. This is not a cry for help. It is a cry for attention, a way of punishing the people they feel have done them wrong. It is a method of punishing themselves due to their inability to accept their imperfections. It is the woman's way of saying, "Look at all my pain, look at the pain you have caused me, why won't you love me unconditionally? Look at how disgusted I feel about myself. I hate myself, my life, and the people in it. Women often carve verbal self-deprecating statements into their bodies. Slut, Whore, Pig, Fat, Ugly Bitch, and Cunt come to mind. These horrible things that they would never ever utter to another person, they carve into their bodies, disfiguring themselves.

While this may seem extreme and not common to all women, the fact remains that cutting is a highly common practice among adolescent girls. This was once viewed as a significant and determining factor in BPD. Today, psychologists and social workers see this cutting among young female women so frequently that by itself is not even considered pathological.

Affective mood instability is the next symptom on the list. This refers to extreme mood swings. Gender difference in mood stability is a well-documented fact. While avoiding filling this book with boring references and citing research, in order to eliminate any doubters here are some of the statistics and research on women and emotional instability: According to the World Bank and World Health Organization (WHO) report on global burden of disease (Murray and Lopez, 1996), in women aged 15-44 (roughly corresponding to women of reproductive age), depression is the leading cause of disease burden and disability in developed as well as developing countries.

One of the most replicated and most widely cited findings is that women are at least twice as likely as men to suffer from recurrent major depression. These gender differences are consistent worldwide (Kessler et al, 1994; Weissman et al, 1996). Higher prevalence of depression is not limited to major depression, but is also reported for seasonal affective disorder (SAD) and dysthymic disorder, but not for bipolar disorder (manic depression) – with the exception of very rapid mood cycling that is almost exclusively found in women.

More women than men have general anxiety disorder (GAD), Panic Disorder, most phobias, obsessive compulsive disorder (OCD) as well as Post Traumatic Stress Disorder (PTSD) (Kessler et al 1994; Kessler et al 1995; Robbins, 1991; Yonkers and Ellison 1996).

Women also have been shown to suffer more from "atypical" sub type of depression, characterized by decreased appetite, motor retardation, decreased energy, anxiety, hyper-reactivity to external events, mood instability, and interpersonal sensitivity, as well as propensity to impulsivity.

Women are also more vulnerable to develop "anxious depression" which many times might be mixed with symptoms of "atypical depression." More depressed women than men complain of feelings of worthlessness, decreased sexual interest, guilt feelings, somatic anxiety, increased appetite, and weight gain.

The overlap among women, of depression and increased appetite, especially under stress, is of interest for assessment of vulnerabilities to both obesity and depression. (excerpt. U. Halbreich, D.N. Nguyen, Impact of hormones and gender on mood disorders, Biobehavior Program, *State University of New York at Buffalo, USA).*

So when characterizing women as moody, it is not a sexist remark it is a well-researched fact. This characteristic symptom of BPD is clearly present in females and hormonal differences play an important role.

As far of chronic feelings of emptiness goes, women have a tendency to be dissatisfied regardless of their circumstances. The need to fill that void is especially present during child bearing years. The intense desire to find a partner, have children, or achieve special status within a career while not pathological in nature, is driven by a feeling of emptiness and lack of fulfillment. Empty nest syndrome commonly occurs in women when their children begin to develop independent lives, and no longer require their constant attention. Responses to this often take the form of needing to have more children, or begin some new time consuming "altruistic" venture that will foster their sense of self-importance.

Intense anger often appearing to come "out of the blue" is a common characteristic among women. This may take the form of "silent treatment" or verbally aggressive and physically violent outbursts. Borderline range often stems from a delusional jealousy and the irrational thought that their partner has some interest in someone else. Occasionally, women even police masturbation in their partners, needing to be sure that they are the sole object of their partner's fantasies. This rage is extremely disconcerting to the victim, especially since in the past they were the object of idealization. This also ties into the paranoid ideation that the partner is looking or thinking about someone other than themselves. This is also where depersonalization and dissociation occurs. The women often feels "out of control" and has limited or no recollection of her behaviors during the rage episode. Trying to discuss the incident is only likely to reignite the explosive anger once things are calm. Selective memory or more accurately a partial amnesia of the event can occur. In its most severe form it may actually result in a "blackout" like fugue state that the borderline has no recollection of.

Early history of the diagnosis:

Borderline Personality Disorder was not officially recognized as a stand- alone disorder By the Diagnostic and Statistical Manual, considered the bible of psychiatric disorders until 1980. That certainly does not mean that the documented history of insanity inherent in women began in 1980. The term Borderline was first coined by Adolph Stern, a physician and psychotherapist, in 1938. He used it to refer to a state of psychopathy lying somewhere between neurosis and psychosis. The patient vacillates between the two states and spends much time right there on the borderline. 1938, is that far enough to go back? Not by a long shot.

Book of Genesis:

For those creationists still out there, have you ever heard of the story of Adam and Eve? I imagine a scene something like this:

The serpent tempts Eve to eat of the fruit of knowledge despite Gods instruction not to. She runs to Adam and says, Oh my god, I am in so much trouble. Adam, you better eat this apple too. Why? So God won't be as mad at me. If we both did it, he won't be so mad. Come on ADAM! I thought you loved me. You're not going to let him punish me alone are you? Come on baby it's tasty, and after we can make love. Don't you want me? I hate you so much! Just try it for Christ's sake! Please, I love you. Just take a little bite, Adam. It will make me soooo happy. And so Adam realizing the woman has lost her mind, decides that living in this constant state of harassment, can be no worse than the consequences God may inflict.

So he eats, they hide. God says, "You can run but you can't hide. I'm everywhere". He confronts Adam. Adam says she was acting all nutty. I was afraid that if I didn't eat it she would cut off my balls. He confronts Eve. Eve says well the serpent made it sound like a good idea. Besides, Adam was off somewhere, and I was really bored. No one was paying any attention to ME! Then that nice serpent came over. He told me I was pretty. He said the fruit was good and you didn't want us to eat it, because you wanted it all for yourself. It wasn't even that good, kinda sour or tart. I was not impressed. And so they were punished. Eve got painful childbirth and menstruation, Adam toiled for food, and the serpent was cursed with crawling on his belly limbless. Eve's curse only made woman's psychosis worse.

Let's fast forward to the birth of Islam. According to the Old Testament Bible and the Koran, Abraham was the father of monotheism. He also fathered some sons. Abraham was married to Sarah. Sarah was infertile and encouraged Abraham to take her hand-maiden Hagar as a concubine in order to bear a child and fulfill the covenant to be the father of nations.

That sounds like pretty logical thinking for a woman. It's not borderline at all, but wait. Hagar becomes pregnant and begins to despise Sarah. Sarah in return mistreats Hagar. With two women competing for importance in a man's life one could

almost see the sparks flying.   Hagar
decides to leave, but God instructs her to
return and to name her son Ishmael. He
assures Hagar that Ishmael will be an
important figure, a father of a nation.

Now imagine this, Sarah gets pregnant.
She bears a son and names him Isaac.
Ishmael was fourteen years old when Isaac
was born. Sarah witnesses Ishmael teasing
Isaac, as brothers will do to one another.
She flips out and goes to Abraham and
insists upon casting out Hagar and Abe's
firstborn son Ishmael.

Abraham asks the Lord for advice. God
actually tells him to do what Sarah wants.
This was probably to avoid further torture
from not one, but two borderline women.
He also assures Abraham that both his
children will father great nations. Isaac's
descendants go on to be the Judeo-

Christian people and Ishmael fathered the people who follow Islam.

Incidentally, the enmity between Christians, Jews, and Muslims dates back to Ishmael being exiled and robbed of his inheritance as Abraham's first born son. The borderline behavior of women certainly has caused some long lasting consequences.

Etiological or Causal Factors:

Daddy Issues:

We have all heard someone use the phrase "She has Daddy issues". This phrase is exclusively used for describing women. Why is that and what does that mean? First of all, all women have "Daddy Issues". In essence, it means that women have lifelong and pervasive difficulties that significantly interfere with their capacity to

engage in healthy, loving, long term
relationships with men, and that these
problems can be traced back to their
relationship with the first and most
significant male in their lives. It is a widely
held belief that males need a strong father
(Or at least a father figure) to instill them
with values, teach them right from wrong,
provide love, acceptance, encouragement,
discipline, etc., in order ensure that they
will live productive lives, stay out of
trouble, maintain stable relationships, and
so on. Well, guess what? Females need
strong, appropriate father figures as well.
But unlike in the case of males, where
their health and success is more cut and
dry in terms of their relationships with
their fathers, i.e. absence vs. presence, it's
a different story with females.

With males, it can basically boil down to
whether or not they had a father figure in
their lives. If they do, that's good, if not,

that's bad. The lack of father figures in the early life of men, is often mentioned again and again in talking about criminal behavior, drug use, etc. The effects of the father figure or lack thereof, is seldom discussed in terms of the health, happiness, and success of women. Yet we know, there must be an effect. It is scarcely talked about in our society, yet the phrase "Daddy Issues", is one of the few signs that we are even slightly aware of the importance of this crucial relationship in the formative years in the lives of young females. This relationship, as it turns out, is one of the major causal factors of women to develop the borderline traits. If we just look at presence vs. absence of the father figure, with the divorce rate consistently hovering around 50% in the U.S., and given custody patterns over the last 50 or so years, that is to say that approximately 50% of girls are raised at least, lacking a full time presence of their fathers. This is not to say that divorced dads cannot maintain a healthy relationship with their daughters, because they can, but it is much more easily said than done.

The family courts and child support systems are without a doubt heavily biased toward mothers retaining custody (I am referring to physical and residential custody, even though most Dad's may maintain joint custody in terms of decision making regarding the child's health, education, and welfare, etc.). Furthermore, even in shared custody situations, which have been increasing in prevalence, where the father may have custody of the child 50% (or close to it) of the time. That still leaves 50% of the child's time without the father being there. And of course the child may attend day care, or pre-school, and will attend school full time by age 5 or 6, cutting the time actually spent with Dad to a mere fraction of the child's time. I have no doubt that the abandonment issues discussed above have their origins deeply rooted in the presence vs. absence of their fathers. But it goes way beyond that. Even with fathers being there every single day, there are many things that can happen in this young lady's life to lead to the borderline pattern, and at best, some dysfunction and impairment in relationships and mental health, and at worse, the full blown disorder and severe unstable relationships and unstable emotional functioning.

Just the fact that divorce is so prevalent in our society is going to lead to another factor in creation of the borderline syndrome. Step Dads. In this extremely common situation, a new male enters the family unit and the household. Sometimes very quickly after dating the mother, the mother's boyfriend is thrust into a pseudo-fatherhood role. While not biologically related to the child, he may be asked to quickly take on parenting type duties. Keep in mind that the mother is also very likely to have unstable, unhealthy relationships, and is probably a bad judge of who would be a desirable mate, based on their own borderlineism, daddy issues, etc. Does the boyfriend use drugs? Does he drink alcohol to excess? Does he have anger management issues? Probably one or more of the above is true. Was he thoroughly vetted via psychological screening and a background check before being allowed into the home? Of course not!

As you can readily gather, the potential and the risks for physical, verbal, psychological, and sexual abuse of this young lady are there. Wow. This is a perfect storm of creating borderline personality disorder. The original parental bond between father and daughter is broken, or severely threatened, and now a relative stranger has been brought in. How is this going to work out? Badly, that's how. I know our readers who happen to be divorced moms are probably thinking that they are good at selecting boyfriends or potential mates.

Well, the first one didn't work out. Did the second, or the third? What criteria do they use? Perhaps is their educational level, having a good job, or how colorful their ink work is? Is it how good they are in bed. Often it is about physical attraction, or because the man views her as sexually desirable, generously gives her positive attention. They are selecting someone who they at the moment see as meeting their own selfish needs. This process works only until they undergo the splitting process, and this person is out the door, or stays on, in a toxic dysfunctional relationship!

Casual Dating to Torrid, to Toxic

As we mentioned earlier, the basis for this work is the years of training, clinical experience, AND personal experience of the authors. We would like to share some of the personal experiences. These are some our encounters outside our professional work. We share these to further demonstrate the main point here. The main point, course being, that all women are borderline to one degree or another. This applies to all the women we've dated, all the women we've known. All the women anyone has known. There are so many factors in our society and in our very chemical makeup that all

contribute in some way to the final
product, no one is immune, and no one
has escaped the consequences.

It's just like saying all males are aggressive.
They are. It is innate. They can learn to
control it. It is a well-documented fact that
very young male children will play with toy
guns over dolls. This occurs even if they
have never seen a gun or a toy gun! How
can this be? It simply just is. And females
will exhibit histrionic traits, emotional over
reactions, fear of abandonment, anxiety,
and so on, which will later make it very
difficult to engage in enduring, healthy
relationships with them. It is difficult, but
not impossible. Borderline traits are there,
in every woman!
Here are a few examples. This one is
completely and absolutely true. Many
people have stories about their "date from
Hell". There is even a television show
sharing the same namesake. Back a long

time ago, when I was single, and before there were dating websites, there were the personal adds in the newspaper.

I came across and ad, contacted the young lady, and when I asked for a general description, she remarked that she is often told she has a strong resemblance to Natalie Wood. Now our more youthful readers may not know who Natalie Wood was. She was a very beautiful actress who died tragically in 1981. Anyway, hearing that this woman MAY look like Natalie Wood, peaked my interest. So, I was excited to meet her, and arranged a lunch date to meet within a day or two.

We met for lunch (and when I tell this story, I'm often asked, "Did she look like Natalie Wood?'). The answer is yes, she did, sort of. Not really, but enough that you can see why people would say that. Truly, she was an attractive young woman.

The lunch date was only about an hour long, it seemed to go well, and so we made plans for another date, an evening date.

A few days later, she agreed to drive to my house (this fact is key, later on), and I said that we would go in my car. When I saw her, I was, well to be honest, mildly horrified. The attractive young lady, with some resemblance to Natalie Wood, who had what I would describe as normal, light make-up when we first met, now appeared wearing bright, aqua eye shadow, several strokes too high on her eye lids. She also had blood red lipstick (yes, it was within the lines of her lips, thankfully, because that would have been a sure fire sign of an even worse psychiatric disorder). To make things even worse than the make-up job itself, her hair was combed nearly straight in the air! This feat of defying gravity was apparently achieved by the meticulous application of copious amounts of any combination of gel, mousse, and hairspray.

When I met her, she had shoulder length light brown, straight hair, brushed neatly. Now, it was sky high, and glossy from the substances holding it up. This was an unexpected turn, which would be more likely to happen on a blind date. But I met her before now. Why? I thought. What happened? Well, very concerned about the appearance of my date, I pushed onward. I told her I was going to take her to one of my favorite restaurants. I took her to a Mexican restaurant in Hicksville, Long Island. It was a lively, popular spot, with a lot of atmosphere and live music. We went in, sat down, and after she expressed a few complaints about the menu like "oh, Mexican food. I don't know if I can eat any of this." But suddenly, her look of annoyance changed to one of sheer

terror. I asked her what was wrong. She
said the men near the front of the
restaurant were bandits! We were about
to be robbed! I assured her that they were
part of the restaurant, wait staff in fact,
wearing costumes, and that we were not
in danger. As her apparent level of terror
and panic failed to subside, I told her that
we would leave, and so we quickly did,
without ordering any food or drink.

We drove away, and she seemed to be
relieved. I drove down the road, to
another place that I was pretty familiar
with. This eatery was a more conservative
restaurant, which I had taken more senior
family members to. It was an upscale
Chinese restaurant. As we pulled into a
left-hand turning lane, about to make the
turn onto the street with the restaurant,
with the restaurant in view just a few
yards away, she started to shout. No!
Don't go there! Imagine my surprise. Not

again, I thought to myself! It just so happens that the restaurant was apparently celebrating the Chinese New Year! There were costumed characters out front! Yes, This really happened! First she was frightened by waiters in "Bandito" garb, and now characters dressed as Chinese warriors from the Ming Dynasty! And they were carrying swords! (replicas, I hope). I probably would have strolled right passed them, and into the restaurant without really noticing them or giving it a second thought.

Ok, I really didn't see that coming, but maybe I should have. Thinking the date had pretty much grinded to a horrible, agonizing death, I drove her back to my house, so she can get into her car, and we can go our separate ways. Probably my mistake, but I tried to be polite and asked her if she wanted to come inside for a snack, and perhaps a drink. Here's where this thus far comic tale, takes a much more somber tone. When I asked her if she'd like to come in, she made reference to the fact that she didn't know me, and couldn't trust me at this point. I, in all seriousness reminded her that she was alone in the car with me for quite some time, and I didn't do anything to violate her trust. She implied that I might force myself on her, once inside.

Then, she bluntly stated to me that she was very afraid that she would or could be sexually assaulted. I assured her that this would not happen. I asked her if something like that did happen in the past, and she replied "Maybe". I knew I had gone too far with my question, and I now believe that the question didn't need to be asked. There is no doubt in my mind in the present day, that yes, this woman was the victim of a sexual assault. Now, everything that had happened suddenly made sense to me.

Feeling terrible, about how things had gone, I asked if she felt comfortable sitting with me in the car for a while longer, and I went in the house, got some glasses, a bottle of wine, and some snacks. She stayed for a while, and the conversation was better, and more relaxed. Eventually, she said it had been a long night, said she was going to go, and she asked if I could walk her to her car (even though it was parked steps away). I agreed to, walked her right to her driver side door, she said good night, and drove away.

All right, so this is a story with a young lady with strange make-up, bizarre, fearful behavior (Until I understood more about her). But, the astute reader may be thinking, Why this example? Even though thus far, it is a good example of how trauma can affect a person, possibly years or even decades later, but where is the borderlineism? Not yet. Hold that thought.

A few days later, she telephoned me. She left a message on my answering machine. For the youthful reader, An answering machine is an electronic device, about the size of a hard-cover book, with a small cassette inside (A cassette is...oh, never mind). It just so happens that the date was about a week or so before Valentine's day. The topic of Valentine's day never came up on our date at all. It did in her message. She began by saying, "Hi. I had a nice time on our date (Huh? You did?), and she went on to say she arrived home safely, etc. and she pointed out I didn't send her any flowers or a gift for Valentine's Day, and her tone began to gradually change...To one of hostility and rage! To cap off the message, she ended by saying "Don't ever fucking call me again!"

A Tale of Two Millies

Before I begin, I want to warn readers that the intent of this story is not to be salacious, but to illustrate the sexual manipulation component in borderline personality, and the effects of borderline behavior on the unsuspecting victim. In this case, I was that victim.

It began one night on a blind date, actually a double date. My friend, John, wanted me to meet his new girlfriend's best friend. All of us were in are early twenties and unattached. We picked the girls up in my friend's fire engine red Plymouth Fury. "It was a hot summer night" was playing on the radio. This was apropos both due to the weather and what was to come. Anyway, we drove to a park after dark. I found this young lady very attractive. She was slim, but shapely, had dark hair that was also unrealistic high, and hazel eyes.

Arriving at the park, I'll call her Millie #1, took me by the hand and forcefully dragged me off away from Millie #2 and John. Meanwhile, John was being dragged in the opposite direction. Eager to see where this was going, I put up no resistance. She pushed me down on a concrete slab near a waterfall. Really, it was more of a drainage pipe into a pond. As I sat on the slab, Millie pulled down my shorts and underwear, got on her knees and began to perform oral sex on me. She did this briefly, and abruptly stopped, pulling my clothes back on. I later found out that this was a "thing" that the Millies did to assess the length and girth of potential partners and to discuss their findings. I guess it's better than a "pig in a poke" as the old saying goes.

She then took my hand and walked me back to the Fury. Confused, but pleasantly surprised, I followed her willingly. Millie stripped off her shirt, when we got to the car, lay down on the hood, and pulled me towards her. In the moon light her supple breasts with her long erect nipples, drove me a bit wild. We engaged in some heavy petting and kissing then suddenly, she pushed me away. She said we need to go find Millie #2, NOW!

We found our friends and the Millie's had decided to call it a night. This was the beginning of a fifteen-month long relationship. Millie would expect me to call her every day, but when I did she would mostly sound uninterested and would tell me that she and her friend were being Millies tonight. This was their code word for we are not going to see you. Whether it meant that they weren't teasing their hair to enormous heights, were hanging around in their pjs, and watching tv, or they were out with other men we were never sure. When they would tell us they were being Millies, they would look at each other and laugh hysterically. If they said they were Millies, we both knew to leave them alone. We speculated that their menstrual cycles were in sync since they spent so much time together. Maybe they were just going to chill and eat ice cream or chocolates. The few times we pressed the girls to hang out on a Millie day we were met with rage full responses "WE TOLD YOU! WE ARE MILLIE'S TONIGHT! We learned the lesson quickly.

When Millie wanted attention, she would make promises of sex. There were phone sex calls at night, and a lot of talk about how much she wanted me. During the entire relationship, we had sex twice. She would ask me to take her out for a steak dinner, and state that afterward we would have some fun at her apartment. At the apartment, she would become sullen or initiate an argument. I was once told that she only has sex with men if they take her to a nice steakhouse.

One day in tears she told me about a history of physical abuse and hinted at sexual molestation. I tried to comfort her and be supportive. At times, I felt like she cared for me deeply, and other times I felt her disdain for me. Being a sensitive young man at the time I felt helpless to comfort her, ease her pain, and saddened and often depressed by the constant rejection. She continually questioned my whereabouts and often questioned my loyalty. Millie would get angry without provocation and accuse me of being attracted to her best friend, my co-workers, my female boss, and any female friend or acquaintance.

Alcohol was very much a part of the picture. Every time I saw her, drinking was involved. Sometimes it was wine coolers, sometimes hard liquor. All of the time, there was a high level of intoxication. I later had reason to suspect that she also had a cocaine addiction and may have abused pain killers. Once when drinking excessively, Millie shared with me that she and her friend went out the evening before Halloween and egged all their ex-boyfriend's cars. I continued to endure the splitting behavior for a long time, partly out of sympathy and partly because of the adoration I received on the rare occasions when she had loving feelings towards me.

Much to my surprise, on the morning of the second Halloween after our first "date" my car was covered in spattered egg yolks and whites. So was John's. I

took this as a hint, and finally stopped
pursuing this young lady. Every October
30, for the next 3 years I had to scrape egg
off my car.

The afterward to this story is quite
interesting. About two years ago, I
received a phone call at my practice for a
potential client suffering from anxiety and
depression. This woman was experiencing
medical and neurological problems. I
returned her phone call and explained that
I was very booked up and could offer her
an appointment with another therapist in
my office. She insisted that she really
wanted to see me. I told her I could put
her on a waiting list and see what I could
do to squeeze her in, but I was concerned
that she needed more immediate
attention than I was able to provide. She
then said that she knew me
personally. She mentioned my friend
John. The neural connections in my brain

clicked. I immediately recognized the voice and said, Oh, hello "Millie", I'm really sorry to hear that you are going through all of this. I could not possibly treat her.

I explained that it would be unethical, and non-therapeutic to receive counseling from someone she had a prior relationship with. I offered her alternatives. She was argumentative. Millie insisted that our relationship was a long time ago and that she would not feel comfortable talking to anyone else. She called several times trying to convince me to take her on as a client. At one point she tried to convince me that we were mere acquaintances. If this was manipulation or an example of amnesia or neurological memory problems, I cannot say for sure. When I refused, she eventually relented. I sincerely hope she found a good psychologist to help her.

As I stated earlier, the borderline traits found in all women follow a similar pattern. It is usually very difficult NOT to find these traits very irresistible. In the initial stages, the men are often told things like, "You make me feel special", or "I melt when I'm in your arms". They often say and do things that feed into our male egos, and our own narcissistic needs. Men must note these "Red Flags", and be careful not to fall prey, unless you do so willingly. Often, women who are higher on the borderline trait then others will stand out. They will often impress you sexually, as they have learned to relate to males in primarily a sexual way. This is possibly due to an early history of sexual abuse. They will strive to please you, and their very intense desire for you will seem very alluring. They may say things like "I don't usually do this on a first date, but I feel such a connection to you."

They will seem exceptionally caring, often placing your needs above their own. It takes a very well developed sense of self to recognize that while this may seem like a good thing, it really is not. As the relationship develops you will see more and more reasons why. Because this individual has such a fragile, poorly developed sense of self, their sense of self will quickly come to depend on you for its very survival. Try and pull away, even to the slightest degree, and you will incur their Wrath! Imagine trying to break up with someone like this! You may feel smothered, and want to run for the hills, but as portrayed in such Hollywood films as Fatal Attraction, Play Misty for Me, and the recent comical "My super-ex girlfriend", you will not have an easy time separating from her.

Dialogue with Borderline Woman:

The following is a bit of a collage of telephone conversations between man and woman. It is all based upon actual conversations and will likely seem familiar to many readers. I must be clear upon the purpose of this illustration. This is not intended to be funny, although the common truth in it when looking back upon your own lives may seem humorous in retrospect.

Man: Hi, Honey.
Woman: Hi. What are you doing?

Man: I was just about to take my lunch break and just wanted to hear your voice and chat for a few minutes.

Woman: Oh I see. You only have a few minutes for me, and want to placate me with a phone call.

Man: What do you mean?

Woman: I just feel like you've been neglecting me. This is the first chance you had to call? Last night you watched an entire football game and barely said two words to me.

Man: Work has been busy, and I don't have only a few minutes for you. It's just that my co-workers and I were going to grab some lunch.

Woman: Oh who are your "co-workers"?

Man: Steve, Jim, and Beth.

Woman: Why did you mention Beth last? What about Mary? Is she going to be there too?

Man: Huh?

Woman: Well you mentioned Beth last like you were afraid to say you were eating lunch with a woman. Are you attracted to her? I know you are in love with Mary now it's Beth too?

Man: I only love you.

Woman: **That's not an answer! And why haven't you mentioned Mary lately. Are you hiding something?**

Man: This is insane. I guess Beth could be described as cute, but I just want to eat lunch. And I've told you a thousand times Mary is an old friend. Whenever I mention Mary, you seem to get mad. Now when I don't mention her you get mad.

Woman: **I just want the fucking truth!**

Man: Yes, I spoke to her yesterday.

Woman: I knew it! I even had a dream about it! In my dream the two of you were making out. Well what did you talk about?

Man: She called me and we just bullshitted about work, common friends, and family stuff.

Woman: Oh, so you were talking about ME??? You were probably telling her how crazy I am. You're such a fucking asshole!

Man: I find it cute that you're jealous, but seriously I'm not interested in anyone but you.

Woman: Is Mary pretty? Is she skinny? I know you like them skinny. And I was just thinking about something you told me two years ago. You said that you love her because she gets your sense of humor. What you really meant was you're in love with her.

Man: First off, I don't appreciate it when you twist my words and use things said years ago out of context. I can have female friends and it doesn't have to be about sex.

Woman: Oh so you think about having sex with her!

Man: I didn't say that!

Woman: You didn't have to! Fuck you! I NEVER want to speak to you again! (hangs up phone)

If this or something similar happens to you, please do yourself a favor. Go eat your lunch, relax and don't take the borderline rage to heart. She will likely come to her senses eventually. If not, you may want to count yourself lucky. This will become a recurrent pattern of behavior. Over time, this behavior causes one to question their own sense of self and can lead to what Freud referred to as a defense mechanism called projective identification.

It is something that occurs in the partner of the borderline, in which the borderline projects her negative feelings about herself on her partner (projection), and the partner starts identifying with those projected feelings.

When this occurs the partner starts to believe that these projected characteristics are their own and may even begin to behave in ways that support that identification. This strengthens the impression of the borderline that her partner possesses all of these negative traits.

As a behaviorist, there are simpler explanations for this phenomenon. When continually being told negative things about you, those thoughts can be rehearsed. Similarly, when treated as if you are an uncaring person, you will eventually start to have uncaring feelings towards that person. So it is important to maintain your sense of self, especially when it is being challenged and threatened.

Let me start to talk about a few long term relations.

Mommy: Dearest Borderline

Many people ask me why I chose a career in psychology. What follows highlights one of the many reasons that steered me toward such a vocation. Of course, since the authors as all humans are born of women, it stands to reason that our mothers are not exempt from exhibiting the symptoms of this plague.

Let's take a look at that. While, we can't attest to the origins of our early stages of our parental relationships, we can look back and recall things we started to realize were just not right. As a child, I remember being generally happy, and feeling loved and cared for However, as I grew, it seemed that the incidences of crisis situations in my family seemed to follow a rapidly accelerating pattern. While I don't think the police were ever called to my home, I do many of these instances resulted in a doctor being called to come over. This was a time when doctors did make house calls, and when faced with situations of extreme crisis, it makes sense that calling a doctor to the home would be much preferred over calling 911. No flashing lights, no sirens, just a gentleman with the trademark black bag, and maybe a cap and trench coat. It was a way to quickly gain some rational, objective intervention, to perhaps a highly irrational and chaotic episode.

I recall seeing my trusted family doctor many, many times, walk up my stairs and into our apartment. Yes, he came over for sore throats, and belly aches, but those didn't seem to be the most frequent reasons for his visits, or at least not the most memorable. One of the earliest memories I have of Borderline behavior, was an episode where my mother painted our brand new Magnavox console television with gold leaf, elaborate designs, right on the genuine wood cabinet. Needless to say, this caused my father to be very angry that his "pride and

joy" state of the art television console was
defaced.

Next I remember, my mother basically
giving herself a crew-cut. Mind you, this
was a poor crew cut at that. I believe she
then had to have a professional "repair"
crew cut so that the hair would grow in
evenly. Neither of those incidents required
a visit from the good doctor. Just a lot of
screaming, shouting, and maybe some
pots and pans being tossed about. Of all
the crisis situations that seemed to be
occurring again and again, there are two
incidents that stand out in my mind.

To give a little background, my mom was
working as a bank teller at the local savings
and loan. She also began to read a very
interesting, yet dubious book about
subliminal advertising. I say dubious,
because while I don't doubt that
advertisers engaged and still engage in the

practice, this booked delved into some questionable aspects of subliminal and symbolic meaning, bordering on the Freudian and other psycho-analytic clap-trap. It even talked about playing Beatles records backwards, which I believe most now consider made up fictions of urban lore.

I remember my Mom coming home from work and getting upset about something that happened while there. "The boss put his coat on top of mine!" This, she claimed, according to her book, was a sign of psychological and sexual domination. Is it? Maybe. Did the boss read the same book and tried in out in real life? Was he trying to discover if it lead to more inter-office liaisons? Or, knowing now what I didn't know then, was what I was hearing the echoes of a borderline split? Perhaps at-work, there were flirtations and maybe a crush, leading to the borderline split.

Maybe this occurred over feeling ignored
one day, or observing the boss engage in
similar flirtations with another female, or
even glancing in a direction he shouldn't
have.

We can't think our parents are beyond
that type of thing. Well, we can think that,
but we'd be kidding ourselves. This is
human behavior plain and simple. Is it
possible that there are individuals that
never flirted with anyone at work? While
possible, it is highly doubtful. I observed a
rage reaction. It seems likely to me that
there must have been an activating event
that triggered it, no matter how slight.
Placing your coat on a co-workers probably
wouldn't incite such a reaction. There
must have been more to it than that.
Anyway, I started hearing more and more
about my mother being the victim of
"subliminal" seduction at the work place.
"Someone put their letter in my

envelope!" Hmmm. Maybe there is something to this stuff after all.

One night, soon after all this was going on, I was jarred awake at about three in the morning to my mother shrieking, running around the house, cursing, talking about God, the devil, the saints, with some sexual references as well. She then proceeded to pick up a hammer and went around the home smashing all our religious statues. Because we were Roman Catholics, she had a lot to get to. She came in my room and with one swing took the head off my St. Michael the Archangel. I really liked that one. It was complete with Satan, or one of his minions being trampled underfoot. I was 14 years old. What was I to make of this? Until then I was mostly preoccupied with the horrible trade decisions made by the Mets (soon after black Monday, the trading of Tom Seaver), or whether or not I'd have enough money to buy a copy of the Eagles greatest hits. Now, I knew, there was something really serious going on. It was serious enough to threaten our mostly peaceful daily existence and all our sanity. Of course, scarcely more than about 40 minutes later, I heard the now familiar footsteps of Doctor S. walking up the metal trimmed stair case.

The same gentleman who stitched up or wounds, took my sisters tonsils out, and had jars filled with diseased organs on his desk. He was a good man, a healer. Now he was faced with something he couldn't heal. I remember us being told to go to our rooms. Of course, we listened intently at the threshold of our doors, and I remember hearing the doctor say phrase I found to be quite chilling. He told my father that my mother was having a "nervous breakdown". Not only did I only vaguely know what that meant, but I had

no idea I would go on to hear that phrase
again and again, only to be replaced by
more modern and perhaps more accurate
terminology (e.g.. psychotic break, manic
episode, etc.).

The next major episode took place about a
year later. Not having a lot of money, our
summer vacations were usually
inexpensive, and just a three or four hour
drive away. This made the Jersey Shore a
favorite choice. I really liked all the
amusement piers, just about a block apart.
So, all of us, thinking nothing but a week of
fun in the sun, amusements, and salt
water taffy lay ahead, hopped in the
Bronze 1970 Plymouth Fury III, towards
the Garden State Parkway. So my Dad
turned on the AM radio, and lulled us to
sleep with the country wales of Johnny
Cash, Loretta Lynn, and Waylon Jennings.
We arrived ok, checked into the El
Conquistador Motor-Inn, dropped our

suitcases on the beds, and my sister and I quickly persuaded our Mom to run out and hit one of the amusement parks.

Upon buying our tickets and walking onto the peer, a ride called "The Lost World" instantly caught my eye. The façade was designed to replicate the ruins of a Mayan Temple, carved into a fiberglass mountainside. It was tacky, but not to me at the time. My sister opted out of this one, but my mom and I were eager to enter. Who knew what wonders and/or horrors were in store? Yup, it was more like horror. But not the neoprene, spring loaded Figures of mummified Mayan warriors that I was expecting. Yes, they were there, but they didn't frighten me a bit. A few minutes (or maybe more like seconds) into the ride, my mom started to react to the ancient ghouls as though they were real, screaming and cowering into the bottom of our rail riding car for four.

Now, I was not expecting this at all, since my mom was also a fan of the macabre tongue in cheek. She had been to many a Haunted House with laughs and giggles and some patronizing facetious screams for the benefit of the ride operators. Her screams became louder and more frantic and soon attracted the attention of the attendants who rushed to the car. They must have seen many a panic attack or reaction of excessive fear given their chosen occupation, but I can see by the look on their faces, they knew this was much worse. Nevertheless, they followed what must have been standard protocol, and opened a hidden, emergency exit nearby, and scurried us out the door to "safety". Their problem was now over, but mine clearly was not.

The rest of the week was in a nut shell filled with my mom hiding under the

covers in the motel room, not really
wanting to speak to us, never mind
venture out to the pool or engage in any
vacation like pursuits. I think we made it
through about three days and two painful
nights and the man in charge decided to
vacate Wildwood and head back to the
city. This, occurrence, needed to say,
combined with the other event, had
shaken my then safe world. Now vacations
were no longer vacations, and fun was no
longer fun. So what was going here? Was it
a panic attack? Not quite so simple. This
must be considered in light of the big
picture, and the central thesis of this work.
Mental illness is pervasive in the half of
the population we are discussing. Whether
it's mood swings, anxiety, histrionics,
depression, hostility, rage, low-self-
esteem, panic disorder, or eating disorders
they are present to some degree.

Let's look a little further down the timeline. Not surprisingly, there were more incidents to come after the two most severe and most shocking. The doctor would pay us several more visits (and we would pay about $5 extra for the house calls). What was to come were several incidents involving crying out and interfering with everyone's good night sleep. The emotional disturbances we had seen thus far now started to manifest itself into somatic symptoms. Screams of "My spine hurts!", or "I have cancer!" would now become very familiar in my household. Cries for help shouted in the middle of the night! Not very different than the "cries for help" that most people recognize as such when someone cuts their wrists or engages in any of a variety of self-injurious behaviors. "I'm hurting, come help me! I feel as though I don't exist! Pay attention to me!" Now you can add health anxiety, hypochondriasis, somatization disorder, and body dysmorphic disorder to the list. But it all comes down to the same core issues discussed above.

Susan, The Professional Borderline:

This is not someone who earns a living being borderline, but a well-educated, health care professional with borderline personality. Susan, a speech and language pathologist worked with me for several years, early in my career. We were employed by an agency treating severely developmentally disabled children in a residential program.

Susan was an attractive woman in her mid-to-late twenties. She had shoulder length, brown hair, slim, of average height and dark brown eyes. Susan would often dress for work in a way that would be better suited for going to the club, than working with intellectually disabled children. Her

make-up was always perfect, except for
when marred by tears. She wore short
skirts, with sheer or fishnet stockings,
high-heeled shoes, and low-cut blouses.
These clothes accentuated a very pretty
body and there were no complaints with
the exception of other snickering females,
who were unable to pull this off.

Susan would often come in to work visibly
upset and looking for a shoulder to cry on.
Her reason for this was always her
relationship with her abusive boyfriend.
He was cheating on her, he was verbally
abusive, he stole from her, he lied to her,
and he physically assaulted her. After
venting and hearing the same advice from
multiple sources she would regroup and go
about her job in a professional way. This
complaining became somewhat tiresome
as she never took the advice proffered,
stating, "I know, but I LOVE HIM!"

One day, Susan came to work in a hypomanic state of excitement. She had gone to a conference on Facilitated Communication (FC) with Autistic people. The theory behind this was that person's with Autism were apraxic and ataxic. Meaning due to neurological issues, they lacked the motor skills necessary for verbal and non-verbal communication. In practice, facilitated communication amounted to "supporting" a person's arm, wrist and or hand to assist them in communicating using a keyboard.

Susan was working with a non-verbal, severely autistic, and mentally retarded ten-year-old boy using this technique. The results were remarkable. Ollie was "typing' in full sentences, using grammar, and vocabulary that would put many typically developing high school students to shame. It began with communications about the child's feelings for the speech pathologist. Miss Susan you are the most beautiful person, I know. You are the only one who understands me. That dress you are wearing is very flattering on you. I wish I could see you more.

These "communications" progressed to expressions of anger towards Ollie's parents. My parents think I'm retarded because I can't speak. I hate my mother, but my father is worse. Please make him stop!

Of course Susan wanted to know what was going on so questioned the child further. Daddy touches me and makes me touch him. Mother doesn't care. He puts his penis in my mouth and does the asshole sex on me. Mommy watches sometimes. The pain is excruciating! Dad is a pedophile. Can you help me?

CPS was called to investigate. Police were called in. As the applied behavior specialist, I was asked to "facilitate" during the CPS workers interrogation of this child.

I was given some training in how to facilitate this particular child, by Susan. All children purportedly needed different levels of support. His involved isolating his index finger and leading his hand toward the keyboard to assist him in finding the letters he was looking for. I felt like a kid sitting at the Ouija board waiting for some spirit to direct my hand. I did try my best to follow her instructions, but all I got was gibberish resulting from random keyboarding. No one but Miss Susan seemed to be able to get this child to communicate anything, much less allegations of sexual and physical abuse. The effect on the family and the agency was profound. The parents were vilified and shunned in the community. Staff became divided as believers, and non-believers in FC. The believers were seen as deluded at best, crazy at worst by those that questioned the method. Believers said that Autistic people could tell if you believed, or not and would not communicate with a non-believer. A non-believer was forced to defend themselves from accusations of not caring about children.

Scientific studies of FC debunked the method of communication. Facilitators were asked to assist autistics in typing a visual or auditory stimulus that was either the same or different than what the child heard or saw. Facilitators either typed gibberish or what the facilitator saw whether it was the same or different than the child's stimulus. Despite cries from believers that the kids knew they were being tested and that's why they didn't communicate, they could not offer an explanation to how they were able to type something they did not hear or see.

This situation was not uncommon. It was occurring all over the country. I would have like to see a study on "successful" facilitator's personality disorders as well as a look at their own history.

Phyllis the Psychologist

At the same time in my career, I was supervised by a lovely lady, named Phyllis at the same facility. She was also a graduate of my school, had her doctoral degree and was a licensed practitioner. Phyllis had always been a very supportive boss. She was an attractive woman and often dressed somewhat provocatively.

Phyllis was very health and appearance conscious. She would have us cover for her when she was in her office, doing Jane Fonda video workouts, Yoga, and other activities to maintain her slim yet feminine body. Phyllis prided herself on running marathons. She would often seek reassurance about her appearance and ask if an outfit made her look fat, or ask about her hairstyle. Phyllis came and went as she pleased. She was highly respected and took advantage of this by delegating her responsibilities to others. Phyllis was a wonderful person to work with, but clearly had some boundary issues.

After four years of having an excellent working relationship with her, Phyllis' behavior became more erratic. She began seeing private patients on agency time in her office. We were in a residential and school setting for developmentally disabled children. She continually made phone calls to private patients as well. Phyllis began testing all her patients with the MMPI, an objective personality test. Phyllis asked me to score and interpret these tests for her.

As an enthusiastic student of psychology, I saw this as a great opportunity to learn

and home my skills. Phyllis was taking me
under her wing as a mentor. However,
after a while this got old. I was being
asked to be her assistant without
compensation, and the work that I needed
to do for the employing agency was
becoming compromised by her practice
demands.

I never complained, until one day. Phyllis
asked me to score an MMPI. The patient's
name and address were on the form.
When seeing the identifying information, I
told Phyllis, I can't score this. This is my
neighbor. Phyllis insisted it was fine. I
stood my ground telling her it was bad
enough that I was given confidential
information regarding him being in
treatment, but I did not want to see a
profile exposing any and all
psychopathology. I said I would happily
continue to score MMPIs for her, but she
needed to leave out the identifying

information. Phyllis became angry with me and never asked me to help her again.

In fact, she exhibited passive aggressive behaviors with me. Phyllis knew that after getting my doctorate I would move on to bigger and better things. Perhaps this contributed to her radical change in attitude towards me. She would give me dirty looks, unappealing assignments, and became generally unfriendly. This culminated in a major betrayal. She was on my dissertation committee as an outside reader. I was told afterward that she never actually read my dissertation, but skimmed through it the night before. During my oral defense she often cut me off and did not let me answer the committee's questions. I was told afterwards that her behavior during the oral defense was sabotaging. I can only imagine what she said after I left the room and the committee was left to decide my fate. Thankfully, despite her behavior my dissertation was accepted with minor revisions.

You are probably asking yourself, how does this make her crazy? It doesn't. It is a backdrop to what happened next. There was much talk around the building about problems with Phyllis and the administration. I just assumed it had to do with lateness and non-work-related activities in the office. Word gets around, you know. I found out much later there was more to this, much, much more. I had left my position to work on a major research study on children with attention-deficit hyperactivity disorder, when I heard that Phyllis resigned.

Here is a summary of information revealed in an article in a local newspaper, lest anyone accuse me of liable (I am also altering her name so as not to bring unwanted attention to her):

On March 14, 2004, the New York Daily News ran a stunning article titled "Sexed-up Shrinks Flirt with Disaster", in which the boundaries between Patient and therapist were crossed in a stunning and bizarre manner. The article began by saying how the therapist would end every session with a hug. And how after one hug, she touched the patient's chest...and then she cut off a lock of her hair and gave it to him..what? Did that really happen? Apparently so. The article went on to say that the therapeutic relationship became torrid and sexual, and they had sex in her office, her living room, and her bedroom. But then the affair ended suddenly after a few months following an argument. He then confessed his "sins" to his wife, and that eventually lead to the couples divorce. The therapist had her license revoked by the state for breaking the field's most sacred commandment. Sexual relations between a therapist and patient is strictly forbidden.

Now, I will deconstruct this unfortunate event. Phyllis had lost several of her admiring employees, her eldest went off to medical school, and the man she married….well was married to her. And as you will learn later in this book, all women want their husbands dead. She had become very focused on her private practice. This for a time, helped fill the void and feelings of emptiness in her psyche. However, the emptiness can be a bottomless pit. I know nothing of the relationship between her and her patient so the rest of this is admittedly pure supposition.

It is possible that the admiration, attention, and affection offered to her by this particular patient, triggered a borderline reaction. She may have idealized him, felt sympathy for him, wanted to be the most important person in his world, felt intoxicated by the rapt attention he gave her. So she hugged him. She gave him a lock of hair. She had sex with him. She acted with a complete disregard for her family, her career, her patient, and her patient's family. So we ask ourselves, why would an intelligent, well-educated, professional woman behave this way? Fully aware of the potential consequences, Dr. M. allowed her psychosis to emerge and present itself in the worst possible place with the worst possible person.

Phyllis was obsessive about her hair. She brushed it for hours on end in the office. She asked people what they thought of it. I believe it was one of her most prized attributes. O.K, I admit it, she had nice hair. Her giving this man a lock of her hair was extremely significant. She, likely, wanted him to have what she considered the best part of herself. When he accepted this gift, I assume this sealed the deal in her mind. Now, they belonged to one another. The over-idealization she must have had for this patient, took over all rational thinking and resulted in this risky and irresponsible behavior.

This should serve as a warning to both consumers of mental health care and therapists alike. Man or woman, regular end of session hugs should raise a red flag. There are occasions when a patient may seek that kind of physical contact, but it likely indicates psychopathology. A therapist must be balanced in maintaining a supportive therapeutic relationship, but still must set clear boundaries.

A male therapist may fall under the seductive influence of a borderline female patient, and must remain on guard for this, at all times. A female therapist must manage the natural tendency to engage in borderline behavior. Female therapists may be able to restrict their borderline traits and behaviors to personal relationships, and if well trained can be a great help to patients.

For example, Dr. Marsha Linehan, a self-professed borderline personality disorder sufferer, created what is considered by many to be the gold standard treatment for Borderline Personality Disorder. So this is not an indictment of female mental health workers, just a warning to understand that sometimes the therapist needs therapy.

I have long since lost touch with Phyllis and hope she is well. She really was a very kind-hearted, intelligent woman, and I am saddened that her life was turned upside down. I also believe in second chances, and am hopeful that Phyllis has found a second chance at happiness, and emotional stability.

The mask of the borderline

The greatest criticism we anticipate is the word ALL in *All women are psychotic.* This seems like an overgeneralization. As a seasoned psychologist, I am always skeptical of words like all, always, never, and none. I will address this critique before publication. First off there are varying degrees of psychopathology. The term borderline, as previously discussed, originated from the idea of being on the borderline between sanity and psychosis. The varying of degree of pathology, does not change the premise of the fact that all women cross the line. The analogy I would like to draw here is how far over the line and how frequently it occurs determines the degree of pathology.

Few women will argue that their menstrual cycle affects their mood, behavior, and even their ability to perceive and respond to situations in a reality-based manner. Men frequently misunderstand these psychotic episodes, and take the psychotic behavior personally. This causes significant relationship strife.

With that being said, women try to mask their psychosis during periods of sanity. The excessive need for acceptance and validation of their worth as a human being drives this effort to mask the disorder. One way that women do this is to take on a caregiver role for those more disturbed than they are. If they can't find someone to take care of they will cause a disturbance in others, so that they can take on that role.

Listen to a conversation among woman. You will inevitably hear one complaining to another. You will hear one woman egging on another. Women encourage one another to rehearse their negative thoughts, validate those thoughts, and provide a shoulder to cry on. When men try to offer solution oriented advice to a woman complaining, women get angry and upset because the man "is not listening to them". By taking turns being the supporter, women see themselves and other women as being good listeners, helpful friends, sympathetic, and valuable human beings.

Commonly, women create disturbances in their own children, in order to be the good mother. In its most extreme form, this is known as Munchausen by proxy. Munchausen syndrome is a severe disorder in which mothers cause illness in their children. Mothers take these children to many doctors, hospitals and treatment centers. No medical cause of their illness can be found. It is often the result of poisoning of some sort. These mothers with their "sick children" receive a great deal of attention and sympathy. The children may eventually die of the "mysterious illness" if it is not uncovered first.

In its less severe form, this Munchausen-like behavior involves manipulating the immature minds of youngsters, thus creating emotional disturbances. Then they take on the loving mother role, consoling their poor children and showing the world what a great mother they are. Dr. Bruno Bettelheim popularized the term refrigerator mother. Political correctness more than scientific study has led to the disuse and dismissal of the theory that coldness, obsessiveness, and mechanical care to a child's basic needs, can be a factor in severe psychological disturbance in children. Dr. Bettelheim noted these characteristics in mothers of the most severely impaired children with autism and schizophrenia.

No one would argue that child abuse, trauma, and neglect have adverse effects on children. This is not to say that all women are abusive or neglectful, just that they subtly engage in behaviors that create misbehavior and high levels of emotionality in children. This gives them an opportunity to soothe the child, or complain to others about how hard their life is because of their problem child. The attention and sympathy devoted to mothers with a problematic or emotionally disturbed child feeds into this psychosis. Conversely, being the only one who can calm this "disturbed child" makes the mother appear to have miraculous powers of healing and love.

Women create situations in which they will inevitably be seen as a victim. I have discussed the tendency to seek out and maintain abusive relationships, but this extends much farther than that. I often hear women complain about how their male partners are uncaring, insensitive, and lazy. When asked what makes them feel that way, women will quickly rattle off a laundry list of offences. My response is generally, "have you talked about this with him?" If the answer is yes it was generally during a heated argument. When provided with a solution of communicating clearly what the woman wants the efforts are most often sabotaged. "Sure he put the dishes in the dishwasher, but he out the plates where the bowls are supposed to go!" "He never buys me flowers!" Have you told him you would like to be surprised with flowers? "If I have to tell him, it doesn't MEAN ANYTHING!" "If he REALLY loved me he would know what to do to make me happy!"

This type of behavior results in a learned helplessness situation among men where they start to withdraw and avoid interaction with the woman. The result is the man is viewed as cold, unsympathetic, and distant; once again validating the women's illusion of victimization.

The Case Studies:

As, I mentioned earlier, this entire work is based actual experience with the emotional, and mental challenges experienced by women, and faced by those who choose to love them (Yes, it is a choice, as is heading for the exits, depending on the red flags waved right in front of your face.). To protect the identities of those individuals discussed within this work, the details must be sufficiently changes, lest a dozen or so women in our nation, will say to themselves "The bastard! He's writing about me". Well, I am not, because any of the particulars, the details of the time and place, etc. will not, or should not ring true. It is unethical for me to disclose the identity, and confidential information I have come to know in the professional practice of psychology. Discussing the lives and emotional, and behavioral aspects of individuals I have known personally, and not professionally, are not subject to the ethical guidelines of the practice of psychology, but nevertheless are subject to my personal code of ethics, and my general embracing of the golden, "Do unto others rule", and the fear of direct or indirect retribution by the "karma Gods". So, with that being said, here goes case history #1.

Alice

Alice has been a patient of mine for approximately eight years. You get to know someone pretty well if you see them once a week (give and take) for eight years. You bear witness to their ups and downs, and everything in between. Alas, as the topic of this writing would suggest, there are many, many, ups and downs.

Unfortunately, far more downs than ups. If the converse were the case, she would probably not have made the cut to even discuss here. But she makes it, alright, with flying colors. Alice originally called the office and made an appointment for "anxiety". After I met her, I soon realized that she also had depression, and much more. Namely, a fairly severe form of the Axis II personality disorder featured in this work. She was 36 years old when she first came in to see me. She was recently divorced, and stated that she was not interested in pursuing another relationship at the present time. In fact, she made some pretty disparaging and hateful remarks about men, such as "I hate men!" Just after the vitriol spilled out of her mouth, it was followed by "No Offense, because you're not a man.",   "Well, you are a man, but you are a therapist, that's different". Why did she hate men so much? What had they done to her? It was pretty much the usual stuff. Men abused her, cheated on her, walked all over her. Now, guess who was the first man to set her on this path of man loathing? That's right, dear old dad. She described Dad as very verbally and physically abusive. Some of it bordered on sexual abuse, as she had to pull her pants down to be whipped by the belt. Whippings came often, for her and all her siblings, without a lot of provocation. Her dad was an alcoholic, often pounding down a couple of six packs, along with chain smoking a few packs of Marlboro, as soon as he came home from work, and sat in his Archie Bunker style recliner.

As you can imagine, her relationship with Daddy wasn't the only childhood traumatic relationship with males in her life. One of her brothers began to molest her at approximately age 7 or 8, and it progressed to severe sexual abuse including intercourse. She told her mother about the abuse at around age 12. Of course, she was proselytized, and accused of making it up. Already, we can see we have a perfect storm of several severely dysfunctional environmental factors. The key ingredients in creating her borderline personality disorder were clearly in play.

It is important to keep remember, Alice just came in for "anxiety", in the beginning. Now, after she finally felt comfortable about sharing all these intimate details of her life (It took several sessions. In fact, she initially denied having a history of any of those severe family and personal issues). She was talking about feeling alone and isolated, very depressed and having suicidal thoughts. "No one will miss me if I'm gone" (Even though she had three children residing with her, who were very dependent on her, and would clearly be devastated should anything ever happen to her). Her preferred methods of suicide that were reportedly racing through her mind throughout the day and night, seemed unlikely to occur "I will drive off a cliff", or "I will drive into a brick wall, and die in a fiery explosion". Yet, the over-the-top, histrionic quality about them was readily apparent. I had to make a plan to contract for her safety. This included her calling me, and calling back up individuals, or even calling 911, in the event she was unable to reach me. During this period of time, I would receive messages in waves, just minutes apart, begging for help. Sometimes, the last message in a series would say, "I'm ok, I'm feeling better, I won't do anything drastic". Then why was she saying she was seriously contemplating ending it all? She was attention seeking, that's why. When Alice didn't get the desired response, and quickly enough, she reported the urge had passed. After all, she really didn't want to be hauled away by force and confined to a psychiatric hospital. Who does? (Some people do, because they see it as a way of having all of their needs met with no effort on their part, but that's a topic for another day.) So, this was pretty much the pattern for several weeks.

One of the major challenges to dealing with borderline traits and acting out behaviors, as a therapist, is not falling prey to all their attempts at getting the attention they crave, and setting firm limits on the boundaries of the therapeutic relationship. Boundaries that they will inevitably try to cross, ignore, and even erase again and again, which will be discussed in more detail to come.

A few months after starting therapy, Alice came in one day and said she met someone. A friend introduced the two of them at a holiday party (One that Alice swore she had no desire to attend, and would not attend). She almost seemed rational and sane as she told me about this gentleman. She talked about how she didn't want to get ahead of herself, and how they mutually agreed to remain

friends, since they had both just gotten out
of long term relationships. However, I
knew that this lucidity in thought and
rationality in action was only temporary,
and in many ways it was an act. Acting for
me, but also acting for the new man, so as
not to scare him away. She discussed
being friends, first, taking it slow, pretty
cautious and reasonable ways of acting.
But she was also saying the things she
thought he wanted to hear, and mirroring
his words and actions. That was until he
fell into the trap.

As you might imagine, things progressed
more quickly than their stated intentions
would predict. They started spending more
and more time together. Within just a
couple of weeks, they arranged for their
children to meet each other, and for his
children, two boys, to meet hers. Hmmm,

does this sound all too good to be true? Then as conventional wisdom dictates, it probably is. Practically a real life "Brady Bunch" was in the works. The idea of a world where a stern look from dad, and a supportive nod from mom, solves all problems seemed plausible. She anticipated a relationships and family life in which no one is ever hostile, or abusive, only supportive and encouraging.

This was a quiet time in therapy. I spent much of my time nodding approvingly, as I heard how well things were going. I did interject some mild calls for caution such as "it's great that things are going so well, but take it slowly, and be prepared if things don't always go as well". Pretty soon, the red flags started flying like after a crash at the Daytona 500. "I think he may be the one." Say it with me now: "Noooo!

"I've never met anyone like him before. He's so kind, patient, understanding. I can be myself with him. (No, actually you can't). He understands me. More importantly, I feel safe with him". (You don't feel safe without him, I thought, among other things). From this point things really accelerated. A sexual relationship began. (Hmmm, what happened to just being friends, and taking it slowly). I must apologize to the reader for my sarcasm, but as I'm writing this I'm recalling seeing this slow motion car wreck happening before my very eyes. As I often say to family and friends: "I'm not one to say I told you so, but I told you so!"

Then they progressed to having all of the children sleep over at each other's houses. The poor children viewed the situation they were in as fun sleep overs, with new playmates, and dinners, and movies, followed by fun weekend getaways. They did not know then, what they now. Well, everything sounds so great so far, but we all know that it isn't, and this is not heading for a fairy tale ending. After just about three months of a relationship, they moved in together. "It made sense", they told me. By now, I met the new suitor, Steve. He was probably brought in to meet me by Alice in order to get my stamp of approval, (Some of the Daddy issues taking place here), which she thought was a lock. How would I not approve of such a wonderful relationship? I will keep silent about my true feelings about this "gentleman". It may come off as unprofessional.

They explained to me how great it was going to be, how much sense it made financially, how well the kids got along, and so on. I also think Alice was subtly telling me that my work was done. She had found her prince charming, knight in shining, etc., and she was going to be fine, and she didn't need me anymore. Really? What about the depression, anxiety, history of abuse, severe dysfunctional family upbringing, and of course, the borderline personality disorder. All she needed was a man in her life, and all this would be simply washed away? I don't think so, and I didn't think so then. But, the current trend line continued at least for the time being. When Alice came in, she repeatedly told me how happy she was. Sessions became filled with more dead air then they had ever been with Alice before. She clearly didn't want to talk about anything, but her current relationship bliss, and didn't want to look past it, or beyond it.

Suddenly, all of the other issues she had just didn't seem to be exerting any impact on her at the present time. Her thoughts no longer strayed to the abuse she suffered at the hands of her father, her brother, or anyone else. Alice soon requested that we space our appointments out. Rather, she stated that she really didn't see any point in coming anymore, and thanked me for the assistance I provided in the past. I suggested that we fade sessions more gradually, both knowing and stating how sudden discontinuation of therapy was not usually a good thing. I knew of many situations where people felt better, then stopped coming, then slipped into old habits, and old issues again resurfaced.

However, after discontinuing therapy, the patients may be reluctant to come back. They may be embarrassed, and feel they may appear defeated, to return, and not be able to handle things on their own, this time around.   So they wait, and wait, and hold off, and resist the urge to make the call, until things fester, and simmer, and eventually explode into a crisis.

 Now, this is what I think might happen with "typical" patients. Not those with severe borderline personality disorders. I don't mean to imply that typical patients need to be in therapy throughout the rest of their lives. I'm taking about patients who have more severe problems, and more chronic or recurring diagnoses, such as depression, or bi-polar disorder AND who abruptly stop therapy. So, getting back to Alice, she agreed to plan visits every six weeks or so for the foreseeable future. Well, Alice didn't stick to the agreed upon plan. She cancelled her upcoming appointment, saying she would call to re-schedule. She did not call at that time. I waited some time after that and I called her. I wanted to provide some reasonable follow-up, given all that I knew about her. I left a message on her machine. She did not return my call. When was the other shoe to drop? I didn't know when, but I knew it would. Of course, I hoped for the best for her, but I had more than doubts that this really was the happy ending of her story. About six months passed, and then the call came.

Alice's return: "Do you do couples counseling?"

I knew it! Yes, I was correct and the call confirmed it. But don't get me wrong, this was not a victory for me. I truly wanted Alice to be happy, as I wish for all my patients. But without knowing anything about why she wanted couples therapy, that request said a lot to me. So, I returned her call, and offered an appointment on her machine. I was happy to get her machine, so I wouldn't have to be pulled into an unintended and uncompensated phone session. I received a call back confirming the appointment.

A few days later, Alice and Steve, the head over heels in giddy love, in the not so distant past couple were sitting in my waiting room. They were sitting as far apart as the waiting room would allow. I could see expression son their faces ranging from a look annoyance on Steve's, to disdain, anger, and hatred on Alice's. When they came in, I asked them what brought them here today, and how I might be of assistance. They looked at each other, and like a championship Wimbledon match between Serena Williams and (Maria Petrova?), swatting a tennis ball back and forth at the speed of an eye blink. "You start". No you". "You start, it was your idea", until I finally called upon Alice to start since she had arranged the appointment. She started to tell me that things were going well between them, but now all they do is fight, he's mean to her children, and so on, until she became visibly upset, and started to cry, and blurted out "He doesn't love me anymore!". He interjected that he does indeed love her, but she shouted him down through her tears, and said "No, you don't!" He insisted to her that he did, and she looked at me and said "He doesn't. I know he doesn't! He's lying". The "Splitting" we discuss over and over in this work, had occurred, and this was the Big One! It was a big split not in the relationship ending meaning, but in the emotional sense, where the object of the borderline's affections, has gone from practically the best man alive, to among the worst. I didn't witness the exact time and date of the change, but the severity of the change is why I refer to it as the "Big Split".

Borderline individuals can experience several mini-splits through the course of a day, or even over a period of minutes. This is the essence of the disturbance of borderline personality disorder, and the essence of the borderline traits dwelling just beneath the surface in every female on the planet. The store that usually

provides excellent service and is a favorite,
goes from preferred to hated after one
experience: "They screwed up my order
and I had to wait there for 20 minutes! I
hate that store, and I am never going back
again!" In fact if, you want to see some
everyday traces of borderlineism, read
through a few online restaurant reviews.
You will inevitable find someone (Yes, a
female), posting an extremely negative
review based on one negative experience,
often stating that they were regular
patrons, and like the establishment, but
now, they are never going bad because of
one bad experience. And the experience
usually has to do with waiting too long, or
someone's attitude toward them, usually
very little to do with the taste or quality of
the food. The borderline woman has no
understanding of, well, maybe they had a

bad day, or the usual waiter was off. No. No, they cannot think in terms of the gray. All is black or white. That would require a process of logical thought, for which they simply lack the natural capacity.

So now I am faced with a relationship meltdown between Alice and Steve. Much like the economic collapse of 2008, Steve's stock has fallen from the record highs, to near worthless levels. And what did he do to cause this? It was probably not a whole lot. In fact, he probably was pretty much the same person. But Alice's perception of him is now very different. She did complain about him no longer being as romantic. Not leaving sweet little notes, or picking up thoughtful gifts on the way home like he used to, but that was part of the courtship process. Now, in his mind, the courtship process is over. There are therapists out there who would maintain that these things should never stop or dwindle. Why do they say that? So the borderline half of the relationship doesn't split! (Even though the splitting would occur anyway, but maybe the lack of romance won't be to blame). That recommendation in couple's therapy is simply to appease one half of the relationship.

In all the years of doing this, I never heard a man say "She doesn't leave me cute little notes anymore" as a complaint. Or, "She won't bring me flowers" (Yes, it's a song). For Alice, the dissipation of the love Steve had for her reflected her deep seated fears of abandonment, and her insecurity in herself, and feelings of low self- worth. He loved me and now he does not. Now he will abandon me, discard me as though I am trash. Without his love, I am worthless, a nothing. Borderline individuals often refer to themselves as feeling empty, or numb, or feeling like they don't exist (or no one is acknowledging their existence, in a way that keeps up with their intense need for approval and devotion form others, and the best possible service in restaurants, etc.). Think of the incredible toll this can and does take on relationships. Even the partner with the highest level of devotion and the greatest intentions, will inevitable fail to live up the standard set by these needs. He wouldn't be allowed off days, or a period of time where he needs to focus intensely on his career, or his family, etc. God forbid, he were to experience mental or physical illness, disability, etc., he would no longer be able to meet her needs, and he would be history in her eyes.

At this point, I will spare the reader a detailed play by play of Alice and Steve's couple s therapy. It continued for a while, and things did improve, but it kept coming back to Alice's issues. In fact, some of her past kept resurfacing to the point that she had to return to individual therapy. Her anxiety and depression retuned as well. She eventually went back on anti-depressant medication. As far as I know, they are still together.

Case Study #2 – Sara

Sara called my office to make an appointment "Just looking for someone to talk to". That is something that people commonly say when seeking treatment, but usually there's much more to it than that. If I gave utterance to my sarcastic inner thoughts, I might say "Oh, so you need a friend. Well, this isn't friends R Us". But, I don't say things like that to distressed individuals seeking help. I understand that people are quite reticent to go into any depth when making appointments, nor do we want them to. But at the same time, part of me wants to call their bluff and say "Really? Then why are you calling a psychologist?'

Now, on occasion, there are people who really don't have anyone to talk to. A few unmarried elders come to mind. They relish sessions because that may practically be their only human contact, at least on a deeper, more personal level. Of course, the goal with them would be to improve their social life with others, help them establish meaningful relationships, or friendships, rather than the somewhat artificial, one sided relationship between patient and therapist. Sometimes they don't have that, and/or need assistance in developing that, so they call someone like me. But I know that this is not the case with most people who say that when they call. Chances are they have one or more of the most common reasons for seeking treatment. Usually it is depression, anxiety, relationship problems, etc. So, Sara, upon sitting for her first session, started to cry, and started to describe a long laundry list of problems and symptoms, using apparent all or none thinking and superlatives in her descriptions. Nobody cares about me, I have a horrible marriage, I'm a terrible mother, nobody cares if I live or die. The superlatives and extreme verbal descriptions one uses are among the most significant of many of the red flags we discuss in this book. Our female readers should be asking themselves "Do I talk like that?" "Do I think like that?". And by the way, as we are writing this book, we are well aware that many or most of our female readers will think, "That's me! They are writing about me!", because we are! Alas, our male readers will think "That's my mother, sister, girlfriend, or wife". That attests to the thesis of this book being universally true and valid. Anyway, I digress. I will get back to Sara.

Sara is very emotional as she describes every aspect of her life being just about as bad as it can get. "Nobody cares about me". "Nobody would care if I were alive or dead". (I will stop using quotation marks for a while because I'm a very slow typist, and this book would have been out two or three years ago, if I were faster.) Surely, this woman's life can't be that bad, can it? Is it true that her children and husband wouldn't miss her if she was gone? Hmmm. This is highly doubtful. However, this WAS her thought process. Also, her negative statements bring to mind questions about her self-esteem and feelings of self-worth. He self- image, as I hypothesized then and I know now, were and are pretty low. Of course, her mentioning that nobody cares if she were alive or dead, triggered me asking her if she ever had thoughts of hurting herself. This is a question, I would have anyway, and for the would-be therapist readers, every patient should be asked that question as part of a thorough intake assessment). Her reply to this question assessing suicidal thoughts was that she has, all the time, and every day. This does and should raise considerable red flags to a trained therapist, but it is not extremely unusual as we stated earlier.

She went on to discuss different plans that she has entertained, and they have come and gone, with varying levels of probability and lethality, ranging from cutting myself, taking a bunch of pills, to jumping off a building, a bridge, and one of my favorites, in terms of the diagnostic value for borderlineism, stabbing myself through the heart with a dagger! Now, unless you living life within a Shakespearean play, this dramatic ending is not a top method that people select for ending their lives. However, borderline women often refer to their hearts, as feeling like they have been stabbed in by others, or they will stab themselves in to end their torment and pain. Note the theatrics of it. I am not saying the risk of suicide is low or non-existent, because it is not, but I am calling attention to the words used, because they are telling. This is how the person actually *feels.* They feel as though they are stabbed in the heart by transgressions inflicted upon them by their husbands or lovers, and they believe that they are deserving of such a fate themselves. The risk of choosing a more practical, convenient and less painful method is there nonetheless (E.g. overdose of sleeping pills).

Sara also told me about her history of cutting herself, starting and ending in early adolescence. Again, this is evidence of the self-loathing taking hold at an early age. Sara also told me she had a history of eating disorders, both bulimia and anorexia, also dating back to adolescence. When asked about abuse, she denied being abused ever, but in subsequent sessions went on to describe a very harsh, punitive environment, and witnessed domestic violence, in which her mother was victimized by her father. She related the eating disorder to issues about lacking control over her life, and eating, or lack thereof being her only way of having control over her own life. (Probably a conclusion she drew at the suggestion of an eating disorder therapist.)

Case Study #3: Marsha's Daddy Issues

Marsha was a twenty five-year-old married woman, who came to see me for post-partum depressive symptoms. She often brought her infant daughter with her to sessions. The child was well behaved and easily entertained on the floor with some toys and the occasional bottle of formula.

Marsha's depressive symptoms were not extreme. She expressed more frustration and disappointment with her situation. Marsha was married to a New York City Police Officer, twenty-years her senior. She described her upbringing as one of maternal neglect and paternal abandonment. She left home at 17 and lived on her own ever since.

She worked menial jobs and cruised bars for older gentlemen who would buy her drinks in the hopes of having sex with her. This was how she met her husband, Billy. Billy quickly formed a strong attachment to her and bought her a very large diamond engagement ring. He promised her that he would take care of her and she readily accepted his proposal. Soon Marsha found herself, not only caring for her husband, but also her in-laws, who fell upon hard times and needed to move in with them and needed child care for their special needs children. She complained about her husband's low sex drive and how she felt trapped. Marsha wanted to carve out some time for herself to go out with friends, have some drinks, and laughs, but this was upsetting to her husband. On the occasions that she did go out, she would drink to access and occasionally recreational drugs.

Marsha had been in before her marriage. Marsha described her first therapist as a nice guy, also about twenty years her senior, who she developed a close relationship with. She said this therapist would invite her to his house for barbeques and parties. He would try to set her up with his friends. She did not view this as a problem at the time. However, when one of these relationships turned sour, she felt guilty about the relationship ending badly and ended treatment with the therapist out of embarrassment. After all, the therapist was simply trying to help her by finding her a good man. When confronted with the idea that the therapist had violated boundaries, and that it was unethical for him to engage in dual relationships, she looked at me with disbelief. After explaining the inappropriateness of the therapist's behavior, she gradually accepted that it was wrong and that she was not guilty of behaving badly. She vacillated from feeling used by him, to feeling like a disappointment to him. She continued to maintain a certain fondness for the man she had hoped would be a good father to her.

So far Marsha's plight invokes much sympathy. This poor woman lived a hard life with no support. She sought therapy and was taken advantage of. Her knight in shining armor arrived it only put her in a more stressful and neglectful situation.

Marsha's situation seems to have gone from bad to worse. Marsha would be required to take care of her husband's needy niece and nephew, her own child, her husband and her cocaine addicted sister-in-law. She was unable to stand up for herself and assert herself with all of these people taking advantage of her goodness.

She grew resentful and angry. She would often engage in heated arguments with her husband nearly resulting in physical violence. During these exchanges either her husband would leave the house, or Marsha would go to a bar. On these occasions, she was often unable to return home without a ride. She often met older men at these bars who made her feel attractive and better about herself. She generally had the sense to get call her husband who would pick her up and take her home. Stating the obvious, the marital problems were extreme.

Treatment focused on developing self-esteem, assertiveness, and trying to find balance in her life, without engaging in self-destructive behaviors. Marsha's mood improved greatly. She was able to communicate more effectively with family members, refused unreasonable requests, asked for assistance from others, and was able to carve out some time for herself in a safe way. However, her relationship with her husband was still strained and she longed for a time when she was free. Supportive therapy continued and we worked on problem-solving conflict situations.

So far, so good, no? No. During this phase of therapy, Marsha was extremely appreciative of all my help. She recognized the mistakes of the previous therapist. She began to describe me as the only person who really understood her and thought I was the greatest therapist ever. Now I may be one of the best, but instead of my ego going through the roof, bells and whistles were going off in my head. Let's review some symptoms: over-idealization, parental neglect and abandonment, self-destructive behavior, volatile relationships, inability to maintain social boundaries, and an attraction to older men? I also was approximately 20 years older than her.

Suspecting borderline behavior, I continued to provide supportive therapy, while monitoring Marsha for escalating symptoms. She began coming to sessions wearing revealing clothing, her face made up, hair styling, manicures, and pedicures easily noticed. She would laugh excessively at my jokes, compliment my appearance and act flirtatiously. Marsha would wear loosely fitting, low cut tops, and bend over to look for things in her bag, exposing her breasts. These distractions were beginning to interfere with my ability to refocus her on counseling. She would speak of her disdain for her husband, his family, and regale in her most recent escapade at the local bar. Her demeanor suggested emerging mania. Redirecting her to be a responsible adult, while also being assertive was a challenge.

After several weekly sessions of this, what happened next was not a real surprise. I received a voice message cancelling her next appointment and asking permission to email me about something. The unnecessary drama of requesting permission to send an email put me on high alert. The e-mail I received said that she was having strong feelings for me, and wanted to know if this was normal. She described thinking about me often and was unsure if she would be allowed to continue treatment, or if it was advisable. I responded that this was a matter that would better be discussed during a therapy session.

The psychoanalytic concept of transference is when someone transfers their emotions for a meaningful person in their life onto another person. Many psychologists believe that the managing of this transference is the key to treating personality disorders. My goal of this session was to explore the role that transference was playing in relation to this latest dilemma. However, as a cognitive-behavioral psychologist, I am not a big proponent of the concept of transference. I wanted to convince Marsha that these feelings were based upon a fantasy of who I was. If I was able to have her accept me as her therapist, and maintain the necessary boundaries of a doctor-patient relationship, treatment could continue, and her ability to manage relationships could improve. Marsha agreed to meet with the following week.

Marsha was extremely resistant to the concept of transference. She felt that this was a way of invalidating her thoughts and feelings. She explained how she "knew" me as a person and that her feelings of love were genuine. Over the course of therapy, people do begin to get insight into their therapists, with the possible exception of truly psychoanalytic psychologists who make themselves a blank screen. Most of Marsha's observations of my character were accurate. I was able to maintain my objectivity by reminding myself of the borderline behavior I was observing.

Marsha insisted that she did not desire to continue a therapeutic relationship. She wanted a personal one. I clearly told her that would not happen and reminded her of the discussions we had regarding the boundary violations her previous therapist engaged in. She responded by saying it would be alright because she would no longer be my patient. We could just be friends hang-out, and see what happens.

Despite her persistent attempts to convince me otherwise, I explained the only relationship I could have with her was that of a doctor and patient. I let her know that I would be happy to refer her to another therapist, and encouraged her to continue her treatment with someone else. She became annoyed with me stating that she did not need counseling anymore. The session ended awkwardly. She did not storm out in a huff. When I told her that ethical guidelines prohibit therapists from engaging in personal relationships with clients for a minimum of two years post termination, she balked in disbelief. This, however, took some of the sting out of the perceived rejection and abandonment.

A week later, I received another e-mail stating, "I guess it's not a good idea to see you again, is it? You don't need to respond to this, but it's really hard for me. I miss our sessions together. If I can't see you, I guess I will take those referrals you sent me." I wrote that given our extensive discussion at our last session, she would be better served by seeing someone new. I provided her with a list of potential therapists, and wished her the best.

Years later, while doing peer supervision with a colleague, I was told of an ethical dilemma he was having. He described a remarkably similar situation with a patient he had several years before. His marriage was failing. His wife was cold and distant and he remembered this woman and wanted to contact her. I tried to talk him out of this reminding him that the reason he terminated therapy was her borderline traits. He questioned if she was really borderline or perhaps was really in love with him. He wanted to see how she was doing and since it was over three years since she was in treatment he did not see the harm in that.

He contacted the former patient, who was very responsive to his reaching out to her and she wanted to meet him. She was excited to see him again, but became impatient about scheduling this meeting. The first time was basically a first date. The woman had a second child since terminating therapy and was separated from her husband. She wanted to know what his intentions were and indicated that she wanted a serious relationship. He said he was not sure and wanted to see how things went.

His former patient insisted on seeing him again. On this occasion she wanted to go to a bar. She displayed her affection for him publically, grabbing his genitals and kissing him openly. She was loud and her emotions fluctuated from angry and aggressive, desperate and depressed, to manically sexual. She also told him that she was no longer separated from her husband. He was confused and wanted advice.

My advice was run as fast as you can. Do not allow yourself to get sucked in. He begrudgingly agreed. He met with her again to break things off. The woman tried to seduce him, demanded money for her babysitter, and finally bit him on his cheek hard as a final goodbye. I sympathized with the therapist. Even professionals can get drawn into the romance and drama that borderlines create. He was able to extricate himself from this, but the temptation was extraordinary.

A Narrow brush with Death

As you can probably tell by now, we have many, many examples of the emotional disturbances residing in each human bearing the Double X chromosomes, the genetic code for being female. We have come to see this in our personal and professional relationships. The following refers to a story convened to me in great detail by a long term, very close personal friend. This particular story may not have even been thought about as being included in this work, if not for the fact that during the most recent weeks that I have been engaged in this project, my friend called to tell me that the following events were recently brought up to him, again in excruciating detail, as though they had just recently transpired. What is astounding, is that the events happened over a dozen years ago, yet they were just put forth in a fresh argument just days ago, and my friend spoke to me and said something like: "Remember the story about my trip to Canada?' I immediately knew what he was referring to, because I heard the tale several times over the past decade, and the fact that it was brought up again, just screamed to become part of this manuscript. It was brought up by his wife, in the context of "You don't care about me! In fact, you don't care if I live or die". And you don't care if our kids live or die!, and I have proof! Canada!".

Now I wanted to make sure my friend reviewed all the important details, so that I may properly describe them here. Here are the events that took place in the great white north, in the summer of 2002. A story that in the mind of at least one person, is the account of a very close call, a brush with death, with all involved barely lucky to escape with their lives. And also the events are presented as "proof", that my seemingly kind, good natured close friend, has utterly no regard for the safety, security and even virtual existence of his wife and children. Hmmm. What horror story is about to unfold? Is my friend someone just like (Insert name), the homicidal, possessed axe wielding maniac brilliantly portrayed by none other than Jack Nicholson in the Shining? This remains to be seen, and you be the judge. So one summer, my friend Jack, and his wife Stefanie, and their three children, embarked on what promised to be a pleasant summer get away. They headed virtually due North, through the state of New York, to Kingston, Ontario. Kingston is a beautiful city, nicknamed the Limestone City, because virtually most, if not all of the older parts of the city, was constructed of limestone, found in abundance in the region. I've been there myself, so I can attest to the town's beauty. The trip was to consist of a mix of relaxing poolside, shopping, and visiting some of the town's historical sights, the major of which, being the 19th century Garrison, Fort Henry. The fort was designed high upon a ridge, to defend against the once thought of as imminent invasion by the neighbors to the South, yes that's right, the Americans! That is not really relevant to the story, but I find it interesting.

Anyway, completely unknown to my friend and his family, the weekend of my friend's visit, the town was hosting the annual, and huge Limestone City Blues festival. A 3-4 day and night event causing the town to swell with music fans. The mile or so long main street in town becomes lively, crowded, yet peaceful, thanks to the Canadian friendliness and laid back attitude, and the very noticeable presence of her majesties' royal mounted police force. The restaurants and bars are filled with sometimes loud, yet peaceful revelers and music fans. That year the festival was featuring the 1960's chart topping Mitch Ryder and the Detroit Wheels which only added to the festivals popularity. Now my friend Jack, who I think is a great guy in many ways, and just like thousands of others in town that weekend, likes to drink.

He and his family had safely attended the festival, and he had quite a few beers that day, I'm sure. The hotel they were staying at was located right on the Kingston waterfront, in the heart of the action. It had live music, and food and drink both in the hotel lobby, and in the street outside. Now Jack, being the jolly avid partier he is, really didn't want the fun night to end. If pressed, he may admit being guilty of a few errors in judgment this evening, for example, maybe not knowing when to say when, and a few others. Stefanie, on the other hand had had enough, was tired, and wanted everyone to return to the hotel room and retire. Jack resisted, and urged the family onward. "Look there's a band just starting across the street, let's go!" After some back and forth, and the kids chiming in with some whining, Jack relented and said "fine. OK, let's go back".

He did however declare that he was the victim of a mutiny, and he later recounted "it was like on *Star Trek (Paramount, 1967),*when Spock takes command and throws Captain Kirk in the Brig". So Jack begrudgingly marched back to the hotel room, bemoaning the mutiny. He got back to the room, and decided he can at least enjoy a Cuban cigar (Yes, legal in Canada), and one more cocktail or beer on the balcony, while continuing to take in the music and the festivities below, albeit from 2 or 3 stories up. While he was on the balcony, he heard some commotion behind him, and he was called to come in and correct whatever was causing the current state of chaos. As you might imagine, given my friend's at least momentary "Kirk in the brig complex", and his admitted state of intoxication, he ignored the requests for assistance, and did not extinguish his cigar, or move from his lounge chair on the balcony". However, the shouting turned to screams, and he heard what sounded like flowing water. He finally walked into the room to find that the carpets had gotten a good soaking, although still less than an inch of water, and the water hadn't yet reached the balcony. Apparently, one of the children had used the toilet, had probably used way too much paper, and clogged the toilet. This, of course, led to an apparently unstoppable gush of water. Now he sprang in to action, much like Kirk assuming control over the bridge and promptly telling Sulu or Mr. Checkov to go to warp factor 7 and get us out of here. He went and turned off the water valve, thereby ending the possibility that his entire family could have met their watery graves in a hotel room that night. He also commanded the second in command, Stefanie, to call the hotel front desk, and ask for a plunger and a clean-up crew. Within a few minutes, a young man who Jack described as being about 17 or 18 years of age, reportedly named "Dudley', and wearing a Naval Captains hat, entered the room. Dudley was holding an upright vacuum. The captain, now back in command, quickly noticed that this would not help at all with the flooded room. Although to his credit, Dudley seemed to notice this on his own, just a few seconds later. Jack wife's description of this as a near death experience, was greatly exaggerated. It was not a dear death experience! A few inches of water in a hotel room is not an event likely to be fatal! You can't call 911 for a few inches of water on the floor! (Well, you can call, but the dispatcher and the paramedics, firefighters, and police officers who respond will not be too happy with you if you do coax the dispatcher into sending them!).

This is a perfect example of the irrational thought processes and behavior that women exhibit all the time. Blowing the events completely out of proportion, and bringing them up several years later! To this woman, with her distorted thinking, she was in a near death experience and left to die. The issues of abandonment are clear, as well as the rage that occurs over this perceived abandonment. While I feel sorry for my good friend Jack for dealing with this in the first place, I'm glad that Stefanie brought this situation up again, as I happen to be in the process of telling the world about the virtual insanity that women exhibit all the time, and their male (or otherwise) companions are forced to endure.

Here's something else to consider. If I were speaking in a crowded auditorium, filled with a mix of adult males and females, and I asked: "Has any man in here ever been threatened by their wife or girlfriend? Have they ever heard their wife or girlfriend say, " I will kill you!" or I will stab you while you sleep! Or the dreaded I will cut your dick off! Or balls! If so raise your hand. I'm sure a great majority of the male's hands just shot up without even a moment's hesitation. Now let's think about this for a moment. Have any males in the audience made similar threats to their beloved females. Maybe one or two of the the audience that happen to be psychopathic deviants have. However, if such threats were made, it seems likely that the police would be called. If they are called, they will come, and probably inform the female "victim" of the procedures for filing an order of protection. They may even arrest the man who made those threats on the spot.

Now, to all the males in the audience who's hands went up regarding being threatened by the females, did you call the police? Why not? Would they come? The 911 dispatcher would say something like "sir, they say stuff like that". They probably won't actually do it. We are the first and only authors to dare to write about what's common knowledge. It is common knowledge that women are crazy. This proves everyone knows it. They are allowed to get away with threatening our very lives and precious genitalia. That's pretty crazy behavior, yet so commonplace that it's completely overlooked and basically ignored. I will have more on this issue later as while this threat may not be genuine the thoughts and desires to maim and murder men are disturbingly, quite real.

The Open Pocket Book or Charge it!

AWAP   Fury & Watson

True or False? Women spend more money than men. We all know it's true. This is one aspect of the borderline behavior of all women that we have not touched upon yet But, depending on your family budget, it may be a huge one. Women quite famously speak often about pampering themselves. Going to the spa, for a mani, pedi, mud facial, or even a massage. It is common knowledge that they do this. And, most people wouldn't find fault in it. "You deserve it", their friends and family members will tell them. But why? Why do they deserve it? They deserve it for just being female? For existing? Perhaps for being a wife and mother. But why do they do this? Women do this as a part of their borderlineism. They do it like many other things. To quell their deep seated insecurities, and validate that they are

153

worthwile and even their very existence.
Why don't men do this? I know there are
some men that do, but the majority of
men do not. Try a little experiment if you
like. Give every man you know a gift card
for a salon for the holidays, or their
birthday, and see how many have used
their gift cards six months out. You
wouldn't do this would you? Because you
know it will be wasting your money. Most
will never go. And it's already paid for so
why wouldn't they use it? Because they
don't need a salon treatment and they
don't want it. Occasionally companies
have tried to convince men that they are
'metrosexual" and should pamper
themselves at spas, but it just never takes
hold. Men are waxing and removing hair
more than ever before, but that's for
women. Women have begun to convince

men that their body hair is unattractive and even "gross". Women have altered their bodies and their appearance throughout history. Often unhappy about their natural selves. Now they've gone ahead and passed at least some of their insecurities onto men, but I for one, am not having it. Why do women lack this basic self-acceptance? Why can't they leave the house without several coats of industrial strength make up? I refer the readers back to the above sections on developing borderlines, including the daddy issues, etc. How many women do you know who would describe themselves as "shop-aholics"? And how many men do you know who would describe themselves in that manner? Women shop to sooth themselves. To quell that deep seated emotional pain that they all experience to

varying degrees. They buy organizers for
their draws, closets full of shoes, blouses,
bras, and sweaters for every day of the
year. And speaking of bras, how many
women use newer and newer forms of
padded bras? Who are they deceiving with
all the additional padding? Only
themselves. A failed attempt to deceive
themselves into believing that they are
attractive, and worthwhile human beings.
But it never really works, does it? What
about plastic surgery, e.g. Breast
augmentation and liposuctions, etc. Now,
greed inspired medical professionals are
often talking about how many men are
now seeking plastic surgery. Again, men
are viewed as an untapped market with
huge upside potential. But the fact is, the
vast majority of men will never even
consider plastic surgery (this is not to

discount men wanting hair pieces and transplants, an attempt to stave off the aging process, a phenomena that grows out of the male narcissism). So, Ladies, keep your plastic in your wallet. It really doesn't help, now does it?!

How Borderline Am I?

As you are reading this, if you are a female, you are undoubtedly thinking, am I like this? Does all this apply do me? If so how? If you are a male, you are undoubtedly recognizing all these signs and symptoms to a differing degree in every female who have known well in any capacity, mothers, sisters, cousins, aunts. You recognize these traits in you girlfriends, co-workers and wives. We all must accept our main premise, that all women are borderline, as the truth, in order to move forward and benefit from this possible astounding revelation.

Take a look in the Mirror

Ladies take a good, hard, look at yourself in the mirror. Does all this apply to you? Have you ever exhibited any of the signs or symptoms we have in detail described here in many different ways. Have you ever exhibited intense jealousy? Have you felt intense anger because your picked up that boyfriend's eyes quickly darted across a restaurant or a store to check out the attractive lady who just walked in, and his eye direct eye contact with you resumed just milliseconds later? Why did his eyes have to quickly return to your loving gaze? His gaze returned to you like a frightened rabbit, because he was afraid of your reaction, of course. He didn't want to be in trouble. He didn't want a huge argument to ruin the evenings dinner date, or the day's window shopping. He didn't want to have to deal with questions about whether or not he finds other women more attractive then you, or even attractive at all. He didn't want to field questions about why you're not enough for him? Based on numerous, punishing encounters with you, he didn't want to go through all that for a basic biological, instinctual response of looking at another female of the species.

If he could have inhibited this response he would have, but he cannot. But, after the initial mechanical, unavoidable response, the conditioned, or brainwashed response of restoring the direct line of sight to your eyes occurred. Why would you be upset about your man having a purely natural reaction and glance over to check out another woman? Are you insecure? Do you have a fear of suddenly being abandoned and being left alone and unloved? Yes, I think so! It is something like that, among other things.

Speaking of Jealousy, a story comes to mind. This is another true story told to me by a very close friend. I can call this story "a picture says a thousand words". The characters in this story are Tony and Tina. At the time of its occurrence, Tony and Tina had been married over 10 years. Tina was always a loving, caring, giving wife, but had a pretty solid reputation as having the penchant for intense jealousy, likely resulting from the obvious (at least to me), insecurity. Tony was an accountant by trade. He was book smart, and good with numbers. He always told me he had an artistic side, well buried beneath his accountant's exterior. He told me he used to be good at drawing and painting, and as a young child, even won first prize on more than one occasion in large scale, New York City art contests. It was all pretty impressive. I never saw any of his art, so I'd have to take his word on this.

One Christmas, Tina bought Tony a then top of the line film camera. Digital photography was already well established, and film photography was basically clinging to life, on a respirator. Bored after years of being entrenched in the numbers crunching game, and with his brand new, yet obsolescence bound camera, he decided to take a photography course that included learning to develop and print your own pictures in a dark room. I guess that would include watching images emerge before your eyes and hanging the prints on a close line, like often seen in 1970's criminal drama films. The course taught students about basic camera operation, use of light and aperture settings, etc. I don't know too many other details about the course, but I know Tony enjoyed it, and he mentioned having musings about maybe being a professional photographer, even in a limited capacity, while of course following the dominant safe and prudent side of his nature, and keeping his day job.

Tony also purchased some basic how-to guides on having a career in photography, and in getting started on actually selling your work. Tony was excited about the potential here, apparently not for the potential spare income, but more for the potential for producing art, and having others see it. I guess selling it would provide additional validation as well. I, of course supported Tony's plan, and encouraged him to pursue his new found interest. Tony's photography teacher, an actual professional photographer, encouraged Tony as well, apparently seeing that he had some talent, creativity, and an artistic sense that many of her other adult students did not possess. She and Tony's how-to guides suggested that he comprise a portfolio, containing various samples of his best work.

After his first course, Tony and a few other students were invited to attend smaller classes with the teacher, where they went on shooting assignments and took their work to a few of the last remaining photo labs in NYC, to further hone their craft, and learn some advanced techniques. While

Tony's portfolio did have the cliché' often seen waterfalls, mountains, beach shots, and some still life, the teacher felt that Tony's strength might be in portrait photography, based on his sparse collection of family portraits, and some pretty artistic shots (to my untrained eye, at least), of his wife Tina.

His teacher, as well as the books, encouraged him to enhance the portrait component of his portfolio by taking more pictures, of various human subjects. Tony's teacher explained to him that aspiring models often are willing to pose for pictures for little or no pay, in exchange for prints that they intern can add to their own portfolios. When Tony told me of these latter stages to his endeavors, I, fearing for his sake, asked him if Tina knew that he was thinking about using human models, Tony replied, "No, she would kill me!" I felt it was my duty to sternly warn him about all the potential consequences of his actions that I could possibly envision, and he said, "It's a hobby. I'm not doing anything wrong". I had no choice but to step back, and have my friend proceed onto this pond, covered by only a thin coat of ice, all the while knowing about the possible perils that lie ahead.

So Tony went ahead, and established contact with a few women interested in pursuing modeling careers, who would sit for shoots in exchange of prints. He eagerly kept me abreast of his contacts, and potential shoots. The first was a young woman who agreed to meet him in a pristine nature preserve, which she suggested would make an ideal back drop for the shoot. She was accompanied by her boyfriend, which seemed to be a good decision on her part, since Tony was a complete stranger. I later saw the results of this shoot, and the pictures were nice. The young lady appeared to be what I would describe as an "Ivory girl". For our younger readers, that refers to a pretty, girl next door type featured in decades ago Ivory soap ads, in which the ladies were labelled as "Ivory Girls". Tony was very proud as he showed me pc versions of the results of his first photo shoot. (He used a film camera, and later had the negative's copied to cd-rom, for easy viewing and sharing. I thought the pictures were professional looking, and artistic, in both color and black and white, with the girl's hair blowing in the wind in some shots, and other "artistic" touches.

For his next shoot, he told me he was in contact with a young woman who had experience doing swimsuit modeling. It was summer, and he told me he was going to meet her at a local beach, to hold the shoot. The model told him that she would bring several swimsuits to change into for the shoot. Tony was very excited about taking this step forward towards being a professional photographer, by engaging in this seemingly professional shoot. He even had releases printed for the model to sign, so that he would legally own the rights to sell the pictures. The reader now may be wondering if he was *excited* by the idea of shooting an attractive young female in swimwear. He denied this was the case. Much later, when he, I, and some other buddies dissected every aspect of this undertaking, he persisted in saying that this was purely a professional endeavor, withstanding the onslaught of snickers and "Yeah sures", form his pals. Perhaps the jury is still out on his degree of personal enjoyment during the activity. This will come to bare a little later in this tale. He did assure us that the interaction between he and the model was purely professional as well, and when we sought salacious details about the afternoon and inquired about the specifics, such as the changing in and out of swimsuits, he told us she used the ladies room. Be that as it may, he completed the photo shoot and as he had done before, took the roll of film to the local drugstore for processing. He also had the photos put on a cd rom for easy viewing, editing, and sharing. Knowing Tina's penchant for extreme jealousy, and knowing how she would not approve, to put it very mildly, Tony was very careful and kept his negatives and prints hidden in locations he believed to be secure.

However, after this latest, and his most significant foray in to the world of professional photography to date, he picked up his prints and the cd rom form the drugstore after one hour processing, secured them in a safe location, but neglected to remove the negatives from the drug store plastic bag. Proud of the day's accomplishments, and feeling exhausted, he decided to pour himself an adult beverage, and soak in his hot tub. He sat there as the relaxing jets, soothed his muscles, only to be given a shot of adrenaline courtesy of his brain, after his fight or flight mechanism was fully activated. The activation of his emergency alert system occurred after seeing Tina walk up to the hot tub holding his drug store plastic bag in one hand, and the negatives in the other.

Busted! He only had a slight inking of what was in store. In the milliseconds to follow, his brain instantly calculated his response, and he decided the truth was in order, and would set him free! After all, he really didn't do anything wrong, and was merely guilty of concealing his innocent activities. The concealment was wrong, but no the activity, he thought. Nice try, but wrong! The reaction he got from Tina hit slammed him as he lay in his Jacuzzi much like the tsunami hit the tranquil beaches of the Tai shore, and destroyed everything in its path! Simultaneously, Tina's eyes shot daggers, lasers, and machine gun fire at the poor man. The homicidal rage was not well hidden in her eyes, her voice, and her

hands trembling with violence because
they were not around his throat. His
pitiful attempts to explain fell on deaf ears.
His defense thought of as sound and
logical just seconds ago, now fell seriously
short. He even thought he could
successfully blame the concealment of his
actions on Tina's own extreme jealousy. In
other words, he couldn't tell her, because
he knew this is how she would react. He
tried to remain calm and cool, relying on
his own perceived innocence to remain
smooth, like a homicide suspect who
knows he didn't commit the murder, and
has an iron clad alibi as proof. "Oh, those
are negatives from a photo shoot", he
matter of factly stated. "A photo shoot?!",
Tina snapped. "Yes, I had a photo shoot".
This was rejected like (Insert NBA star)
emphatically blocking a shot. Is this your

girlfriend? How long have you been seeing her? "You disgusting, lying, piece of shit. You make me sick, I hate you!" Tina's rage quickly turned to heartbreak, as the waterworks began to gush. "How could you do this to me, the mother of your children." She turned and ran into the house.

Wait! He shouted, I can explain, I didn't do anything wrong! But she was not upset about a modeling shoot, she thinks he was unfaithful. That was going to be a major problem convincing her otherwise. He said everything he could in his defense, as fast as he could get the words out. After over an hour of dealing with alternations between sobbing and cursing, switches between divorce threats and death threats, he finally started to make some headway. At least on the infidelity charges, she began to relent. He produced evidence supporting his claim that this was a photo shoot. He remembered the signed release! It was irrefutable proof, he thought. After a few hours, calm finally began to roll in. Questions were asked and answered. Things seemed to be clearing up. Tina told him that there was a lot she needed to digest. She told him that she needed some space and time to think, he obliged, and she went into another room to watch television. She fell asleep after her outbursts lead to her exhaustion. He thought he had weathered the storm and was now in the clear.

Tony was wrong again. She woke up from her nap hours later, and then he was hit with the second wave of the tsunami. She marched up to him, got in his face and said, "How many times did you f----k her?!" He emphatically denied that he did. Annoyance and surprise in his voice that this was not over at this point. She insisted that he tell her the number of times they had sex. How was it? Did she go down on you? She referred to the young lady as a slut, and a whore. His repeated unwavering denials appeared to ever so gradually gain some credibility. She was calmer again. There were more questions. Did she change in front of you? Did you see her naked? Where did you meet her? How were these arrangements made? Did you pay her? How much? Will you see her again?"

Again, the situation seemed to be resolved. Yet Tony told how this cycle continued, lessening slightly at each occurrence, but repeating itself, day after day, week after week. With some very gradual reduction in the frequency of the occurrences, Tony used to tell me when this whole situation was brought up again. I no longer ask him about it, since it happened so long ago. But I'm sure the potential remains there for it to be brought up during an argument, or should any suspicions arise. Also, Tony was forced to give up all his photography aspirations. He was repeatedly told that Tina married an accountant not a photographer, and that she would not stay married to him unless he promised to quit. I think this was a pretty good example of many of the issues we had previously discussed. The borderline rage, the insane jealousy, the deep rooted insecurity are all undeniably evident in this case. I hope Tony continues to behave himself! Artistic expression is forbidden in his life.

Creativity is contraband. Dreams must be abandoned! Or else! While this is an example of how Tony knowingly strayed from the rules, think of how careful he must be on a daily basis, in order to avoid setting his wife off. Even a glance towards an attractive woman might trigger and episode that Tony clearly wishes to avoid. Walking on egg shells forever is his current life sentence!

Women of other cultures

By now, you should be totally convinced about the disordered nature of every woman's emotional and psychological make-up. But, we have focused on the women we know best, American women. The fact, however, is that the borderline disordered nature of all women transcends all borders, boundaries, and cultures on planet earth. I myself can boast that I have been lucky enough to date women who are of diverse ethnic and cultural backgrounds. The following is a true account of my experience with one of those ladies.

I have a close friend who has always been drawn to dating ladies from the far-east. Ladies of Asian heritage is his preference. This buddy of mine was dating a Korean lady at the time, and they decided to invite an Asian co-worker to my home as a fix-up. Let's call the lady Kim Su. She, Brian, and his girlfriend came over one evening, and we had some take out (Chinese I believe) and some cocktails. Kim Su was very attractive. She was half-Chinese and half Japanese, and this combination of genetic material had led to the creation of quite an excellent female specimen. She had long, jet black silky hair flowing down to the middle of her back. And, oh, what a back that was. She was thin and petite, yet curvy in all the right places.

At the time of our meeting, she was barely able to speak English. Throughout the evening I made silly jokes, which she probably barely understood, but they all seemed to hit the target and resulted in her feminine, delicate laughter or a the very least resulted in her shy smile. Just a couple of hours into the evening, and likely assisted by the social lubrication provided by my excellent mixology skills (martinis, margaritas, Pina coladas? I don't know, I can't recall. Even though we couldn't verbally communicate very well, I sensed a mutual attraction. I guess you can say we spoke Amore, the language of love.

To the amazement of my compadre, I got up, stepped towards her, and took her by the hand back to where I was sitting. I gently guided her to sit on my lap, which she did without a trace of resistance, and we started to kiss. My friend was shocked and hopefully impressed that we transcended our language barrier and quickly moved to making out, in less than a couple of hours. Soon after, we decided to conclude our evening, as Kim Su's girlfriend had to drive her back to the city. I did get her digits and called her after waiting the requisite 2-3 days.

We arranged a date, and I picked her up, and we went for dinner at one of her favorite restaurants (Asian, of course). We stammered through our conversation with vocabulary probably hovering the 2-3 year old developmental level.

After dinner, she invited me up to her apartment. Soon after walking in, she said something like "Wait, here please..I change." She returned a few minutes later, and it was readily apparent that she was wearing nothing but a silky, floral patterned robe. She motioned for me to enter her boudoir, and well, since this is not one of those soft-core novels du jour, I will just say we became intimate. I do think it is relevant to say, however, that she did offer what I would call "The full Geisha treatment", that included a sensual massage, and even included a hot towel treatment when the intimacy part concluded (wait, I know what you're thinking..and stop it! She was a professional...no not that kind of professional! She was in finance!)

But wow! I thought. This was great. I'm sure I left with the classic ear to ear smile telling the world what I just experienced.

Next after stumbling through a few phone calls over the next few days, we talked about spending the impeding New Years Eve together. I didn't have any plans, and I thought an "intimate gathering" would be much more enjoyable to me, than the standard, crowded, night club or even house party experience. I was right..sort of.

We decided to have take-out (Sushi I recall, and I'm pretty positive about that). Watched some movies and standard New Year's Eve fare, and we again resumed where we left off (or I should say repeated) our physical relationship. And it was very, very good. However, when she reached a certain point of physical pleasure (modesty prevents me from describing further), she (while we were still "coupled" so to speak"), began to strike me. She pounded my chest and shoulders repeatedly with her fists. I was astounded!

I blocked what I could, and eventually grabbed her arms, and told her to stop, but she wouldn't. Every time her hands were freed, the onslaught continued. She finally stopped after what were several painful minutes for me, and basically threw herself into a fetal position on the floor in the corner of the room, and began to weep uncontrollably.

What the hell just happened? I thought. How crazy is she? What childhood trauma or daddy issues did I just bring to the surface via my lady pleasuring skills? And how could my New Year's Eve turn so shitty, so fast? The crying continued unabated for probably over an hour. I tried to console her, but had to threaten her

with having to leave if she did not stop.
She eventually did, repeatedly said sorry,
and after I while we agreed it would be
best if she did go home for the night.

Kim Su called me the next day. She acted
like none of that madness ever happened.
She asked me when she would see me
again. Am I as crazy as she is? Should I
even consider seeing her? She made the
decision easy for me. She asked me if I can
come to her job soon. Her job? Why? She
said she wanted her co-workers to meet
me. Why? I asked. Then she dropped the
b-word on me. That's right. She said that I
am her BOYFRIEND! And that she wants to
introduce me to her co-workers. What?
Even if I was her B-B-B- Boyfriend, there is
absolutely no reason to meet her co-
workers. (I guess it's a cultural thing, or
something, but I have no idea.).

Well, using the b-word on me was disturbing, especially since I was thinking she was absolutely nuts. So I had to set her straight. I told her I liked her, but that I wasn't her boyfriend, since we practically just met. She seemed slightly upset and somewhat startled by this news, but maybe she didn't even really understand what I was saying to her. She asked again about coming to meet her co-workers, and I told her I wouldn't be doing that. After some minutes of awkward silence, the conversation ended. The next day, I came home, and pressed the play button on my answering machine (yes, the same one I mentioned earlier), and in her stuttering broken English told me I hurt her so badly, and she never wanted to see me again! Oh, well, there goes that!

Note from co-author: Cultural aspects and implications that should be addressed.

1. *The Beginning of the New Year is highly significant in Asian culture. What happens on the evening and first day of a new year is considered a portent of the remainder of the year. This is the reason casinos are filled on Chinese New Year. Superstition regarding luck and future events is no more important than on the day of Kim Su's psychological break down.*

2. *Since Kim Su's orgasm on the most significant day of the year was a portent of continuous orgasms with this man, that she hardly knew, Kim Su needed to find some greater significance to this sexual encounter, namely being her boyfriend. Thus, my esteemed co-author was place in*

*a position of importance, and it was
time to meet the family (co-workers).*

Neither of these cultural factors negates
the psychosis experienced by Kim Su. It is,
however, important to note that various
cultural factors may be specific triggers for
psychotic responses for women of
differing cultural backgrounds.

Why All Women Want Their Husbands Dead

This may sound like an absurd or
sensational statement, however after a
certain time in a marriage the
development of these homicidal thoughts
is inevitable. The vast majority of women
do not overtly act on those thoughts, but
nearly all will engage in passive-aggressive
or overtly aggressive behaviors when
overcome by feelings of intense anger.

I cannot even tell you how many times in a therapy session a married woman, always with children, has told me, " I wish my husband was dead." or I'd really like to kill my husband." , or "I dreamt I killed my husband". When a patient expresses suicidal or homicidal ideation, I generally do a complete risk assessment and if necessary warn the potential victim. When it is the wife talking about her husband, my level of concern is greatly reduced. That is not because I am not concerned about my duty to warn someone of imminent danger. It is because of the amount of husbands I would need to call to tell them what they already know. Also, violating confidentiality would undermine the trusted therapeutic relationship and result in greater risk.

I generally ask about intent. "I understand that you have thoughts about killing your husband, but do you really think you might do it?" The answer most often is an emphatic no, I would never. At that point, my concern is greatly diminished. I address the thoughts and feelings that trigger the urge to harm the spouse. Just in case you are wondering, I have never had a man in treatment say "I want to kill my wife." If I did I would be extremely concerned, even physically abusive husbands, do not generally express homicidal ideation. They have severe anger management problems and personality disorders, and are difficult to treat. I worry about those people causing physical harm or death, actually more than the women that verbally express a desire to do away with their man. There is a social acceptability to women verbalizing thoughts of hating or wanting to murder husbands. People are not shocked to hear this. But why do women fantasize about killing their husband or seeing them dead? In my experience as a clinician many reasons have emerged.

First off, men cannot live up to the idealized image the borderline woman generates when they "fall in love". She expects prince charming to provide for, protect, adore, and attend to her every need. She deceives herself into believing that this man is the ONE TRUE LOVE! With that, comes magical thinking. The man is all powerful, yet sensitive, and caring. He knows me as well or better than I know myself. He will never lie to me. He will never leave me. He will never look at or desire another woman. I will bear his children and they will be amazing, because his seed is good. He will be a devoted father, and always pay close attention to me. Women develop and hold on to these irrational beliefs early in the relationship. These beliefs are so strong that the man they are with becomes intoxicated by the adoration he receives, and begins to feel he can do no wrong.

And yet men are unable to read minds, or know what a woman wants before she wants it. I often hear women say, but if he really loves me he should know what I want without me telling him. He is often incompetent and unable to resolve problems in a heroic manner. Circumstances are often too challenging for a man to be successful. Men can be self-centered and forget important events in a woman's life. Men make mistakes, act foolishly, get frustrated, can suffer from depression, have fears, get hurt, suffer from illnesses. Heterosexual men also enjoy the attention of women. They find women sexually attractive, look at them, fantasize about them sexually, and sometimes act on these impulses for sexual and emotional gratification.

Prior to having children, couples lives are much simpler. It is thus easier for the man to meet the many expectations, and for the women to overlook it when the man falls short. Also, the woman's biological imperative to procreate places creates a stronger hold on the over-idealization of the man. Women do not want to have doubt that they found the correct mate to give them children. They may reject a man early in a relationship if they do not find him as an appropriate mate. This is an instinctual behavior in the entire animal kingdom.

After having the desired number of children, the man's value diminishes. The veil of awesomeness is lifted. Superman becomes Clark Kent, Spiderman turns into Peter Parker, The Hulk is really only Bruce Banner.

Now the woman begins to question. Why are these strongly held positive beliefs being contradicted by reality, or their new perception of reality? A female therapist engaged in couples counseling was attempting to mediate a dispute. The husband called out the wife regarding a distortion of what took place. The husband stated that's the way you perceived it at the time, but it's not what actually happened. The therapist became visibly angry and shouted, "Perception is reality!" Clearly the therapist's own borderline traits came into play when identifying with the woman.

Aspects of borderline personality previously discussed include transient dissociative symptoms. Dissociation is by definition a break from reality. It includes depersonalization or feeling outside of oneself, memory loss, and de-realization or a feeling as if one is not part of the real world. This common symptom among borderlines is an example of the fragile nature of the grip women have on reality.

Now imagine, everything you believed about this man turning out to be false.

This creates a situation psychologists refer to as cognitive dissonance. This is simply the discomfort one feels when faced with two opposing beliefs. Splitting is the most extreme example of cognitive dissonance. Over-idealization contradicted by devaluation causes extreme discomfort which must be resolved in order for the woman to function. So women may seek to justify the positive belief they are currently holding by finding reasons for, or excusing the man's imperfect actions based upon some situation out of his control. Alternatively, she may deny or ignore the man's imperfect behavior in order not to experience cognitive dissonance.

Eventually, these strategies fail. Since men as all humans are imperfect beings, continued failure to meet the idealized

standard set for them becomes too much
for the woman to bear. So, we get back to
the question "why women fantasize about
the death of their husbands". When faced
with this cognitive dissonance, and the
failure to maintain a positive belief about
the man, they must justify the opposing
belief. One way, is "He deceived me!"
Women begin to believe that there was an
elaborate plan to convince the woman
that he was all the things she dreamed he
would be.

Now the man is a liar, a deceiver, a
manipulator. I have heard many a woman
in counseling and personal life tell me,
"This isn't what I signed up for, when I
married him", or "He's not the same man I
married", or "I don't even know who he is
anymore". Sound familiar? The woman
now feels that her life was stolen from her.
The man is a thief. The woman goes over
all the things she ever did for the man,
with intense resentment. I gave him love,

adoration, cared for him. I gave him my body sexually, I gave him the best years of my life, but he wasn't the man I thought he was. It was all a lie, a disguise, a trick!

A second way to manage the discomfort of the cognitive dissonance is to abandon the positive beliefs all together, by extreme devaluation. In this case, the woman will blame herself for ever holding the positive belief in the first place. The all or nothing thinking, however takes hold and now the woman **realizes** her man is a loser, pathetic, unattractive, weak, stupid, overbearing, needy, hateful, untrustworthy, void of compassion, sexually impotent, a burden of the utmost proportion.

Is it any wonder that women want their husbands dead? Even without true intent women develop elaborate fantasies on how they would kill their husbands. Poisoning food comes to mind.

Sometimes women take action and engage in what I would call homicidal gestures. One patient of mine asked her 21 year old daughter to lick her father's glass when she had 103 degree fever and strep-throat. Another woman I treated who felt unloved by her husband because he lost interest in sex, admitted to swiping his toothbrush around the toilet bowl every morning. I have heard on several occasions from friends that their wives actually stated they wanted to stab their husbands in the heart while they slept. I have not heard that in counseling, because most women know that kind of threat would be taken quite seriously and could result in their hospitalization.

Men are also often the victims of domestic violence. This goes unreported most of the time. Non-abusive men have been taught that you NEVER strike a woman. Boys are also taught the most emasculating event is to get beat up by a girl. The embarrassment, shame, and fear of retribution make many men the perfect victims. Many times these gestures are simply passive aggressive behaviors. Deliberately engaging in behaviors, or not doing everyday things that will cause inconvenience to the man. This causes chronic stress and is also detrimental to the man's health.

In conclusion, the reason why women want their husbands dead is that the women find that their husbands are no longer deserving of their over-idealization. The feeling of being with the "man of her dreams" is lost. That feeling is essential to the woman's feeling of fulfillment. It is a drug, a high that can be compared to no other. The husband is now an obstacle in the way of achieving that high. Only in his death will she be truly free to once again experience what she once had with him. Gentleman, sleep with one eye open.

Steps in developing the disorder:
Borderline behavior in girls can be seen at
an early age. Psychological gender
differences are readily apparent. As early
as Kindergarten, boys and girls begin to
develop a pecking order socially. Girls
tend to display a much more dramatic
approach than boys. We see a
competition for attention and acceptance
that often has a Machiavellian quality
among girls. They tend to create conflict
among their peers, tell tales, and display
dramatic emotional reactions when they
are not the center of attention. Boys on
the other hand, tend to fight over things,
or leadership. Usually the physically
stronger or more intelligent child wins the
desired object or leadership role, and the
weaker one accepting his loss, albeit with
great sadness or disappointment. Not so
with girls, there is a constant social drama
being played out. Girls seek ways to
isolate other girls from friendships while

trying to solidify their place in the social hierarchy. The intense need for love and acceptance by peers often results in friends demonizing other friends, causing hurt feelings, intense anger and depression.

It is theorized that Borderline Personality Disorder is a result of severe physical, emotional, and/or sexual abuse in childhood. While these factors certainly exacerbate the disorder, I assert that they are not causal in nature. The only necessary condition is being female. This is also a sufficient condition. At risk of a future splitting reaction once my daughter reads this tome, I will tell my personal story.

My own daughter currently eleven years old, displayed some of many of the dramatic characteristics, from an early age. Rest assured she did not experience any traumatic events or abuse in her life, and was if anything "spoiled" as the first born child.

My first girl came into this world in a very dramatic fashion. Upon birth, the screams and howls began. My daughter was beautiful, but inconsolable about being forcibly removed from the peaceful quiet of her mother's womb. She was born by Caesarian section. Madison was a healthy baby, no colic, ear infections, or other significant medical problems. However, she was not an easy baby.

Being a new parent, despite being a behavioral psychologist, I made some mistakes. Not wanting to hear my lovely baby daughter cry, I would rock her to sleep as I sung her sweet lullabies. As soon as I attempted to lay her in her crib, the crying would resume. Hours spent each night trying to get her to sleep had become exhausting. One day I realized my behavior was contributing to the problem. While I knew all about the Ferber method and am a behaviorist by nature, I seemed to forget the basics when it came to my own child. Once employing techniques of planned ignoring my daughter learned to self soothe.

In order to preserve my wife's tenuous grip on sanity, I would often place her in the Baby Bjorn and walk with her strapped to my own chest for miles. Her demanding nature and low frustration tolerance were too much for my wife to handle at times. I realize babies are difficult, but Madison was giving me a glimpse into what was to come.

I must say at this point that I adore both my daughters equally. They are kind hearted, intelligent, and funny children. I only pick on Madison now, because she is the better example of how all women are crazy. Sophia, my younger daughter has tendencies, but they are not as dramatic or as extreme.

Even in preschool and Kindergarten, "Maddy" would come home with tales about how another child was mean to her, how the teacher didn't respond to some conflict the way she "should" have. She even once mutilated a school photo by drawing over faces of children whom she felt treated her unfairly. The social drama has continued to this day.

Tantrum behaviors at home were common and continue to be. Splitting is frequent. I am often loved and told I am the best Dad ever and just as often hated and told that I am the worst father in history! The same is true for my wife. Madison can be the sweetest child and people outside the immediate family cannot believe that she acts the way she does at home.

Her little sister, Sophia, entering second grade now, adores Madison and looks up to her. Sophia has written journal entries and stories about how she loves her sister and wishes she would be nice to her again. The illustrations are heartbreaking depictions of Sophia crying, while Madison yells at her saying that she hates her. It brings back memories for me of my own older sister treating me poorly. My sister's insanity is worthy of a chapter, or perhaps a book herself.

Madison exhibited intense and sudden mood swings from an early age. So it was no surprise to me when on my fiftieth birthday Madison, three months shy of her tenth birthday, had her first menses. It was as if to say, you thought it was bad before...haha. When in a foul mood,

Madison will often look for an argument. She argues relentlessly and takes the opposing side of any argument taken. These intense tantrum- like behaviors do not respond well to punishment.

While planned ignoring is the best course of action, it is difficult to implement consistently. The intensity of the behavior becomes quite extreme and difficult to ignore. In addition, there are two other females in the house that are likely to respond to the escalation.

Despite my behavioral background, I do not believe planned ignoring in these situations is the best course of action solely because I am trying to extinguish an undesirable attention-seeking behavior. I believe that the function of the behavior is a hormonal imbalance causing a neurological failure to engage in rational thinking. Simply put, her brain is incapable of reason during these episodes. Planned ignoring under these conditions is simply a way of riding out the emotional storm.

There is no need to go into any specific examples of situations, because the antecedent events are generally irrelevant to the behavior. These storms develop from a clear blue sky. I have learned not to take anything said or done during these episodes personally, and I know when they are over my lovely sweetheart of a daughter will return.

Now, Go Ahead and make our day! Take our test!

We have developed a self-report questionnaire to help determine levels of borderline (female) psychosis. This test is

intended to identify and rate the severity
of the disturbance.

The Test of Borderlineism

I identify myself as a female.   t/f

I like the color red.   t/f

The story of Adam and Eve is true. t/f

I believe in Ghosts.t/f

I have seen a ghost.   t/f

I have had thoughts of hurting myself.   t/f

Evil spirits are real.   t/f

People often tell me to relax.   t/f

Sometimes I see spots.   t/f

My relationships are stormy.   t/f

I have nightmares.   t/f

I watch soap operas.   t/f

I watch talk shows hosted by females. t/f

I own more than a dozen pairs of shoes t/f

I have cut myself.   t/f

I dream in Vivid Colors: t/f

I have dated more than a dozen men. t/f

I would like to meet my knight in shining armor.

I have tried to kill myself. t/f

I use sleeping pills. t/f

I love Romantic Comedies,   t/f

I can't handle break ups. t/f

I have trouble sleeping at night.   t/f

I cry often.   t/f

I often feel lonely. t/f

I have made threatening remarks to other in
anger (Even if I wouldn't act on it).

I go shopping when I'm feeling down. t/f

I am a spiritual person.   t/f

I often feel like no one cares about me. t/f

I don't like my body.   t/f

I have trouble concentrating at school or work.
t/f

I drink alcohol to excess.   t/f

I would like to ride on the back of a motor cycle.
t/f

I have frequent headaches.   t/f

I have frequent stomach problems. t/f

I have very difficult periods. t/f

I experience PMS. t/f

I wear sexy costumes on Halloween.   t/f

I eat excessively when I'm feeling down. t/f

People often tell me to me to calm down. t/f

I have broken objects in anger. t/f

Friends tend to let me down. t/f

The world is a frightening place. t/f

I call my friends more often than they call me. t/f

I get upset when people don't treat me with respect. t/f

My friends and family can always count on me t/f

People rarely give me the respect I deserve t/f

People don't really understand me t/f

My parents didn't' show me enough love t/f

If you answered true to number of items:

0-19 : Mild Borderline Traits (among the lowest scoring females)

20-29: Significant signs of neurosis

30-39: Borderline Personality

40 or more: Bat-shit crazy (seek immediate assistance)

Sadly there is no cure for Borderline Personality Disorder, any more than there is a cure for femaleness. However, in women who express severe symptoms, multi-modal treatment can be effective in minimizing the disorders effects. Identification and treatment of Borderline Personality Disorder is imperative.

Initially, comprehensive evaluation by adequately trained and skilled mental health providers is most important. It is not enough to recognize borderline traits, but also to identify disturbed patterns of behavior and co-morbid mental illness. What makes this disorder so debilitating is the affective and behavioral excesses, which often cause misdiagnosis and missed diagnoses. As previously mentioned, depression, anxiety, PTSD, eating disorders, histrionic personality disorder, intermittent explosive disorder, bipolar disorder, dissociative disorders, and many other common psychiatric disorders and symptoms overlap or coexist within the Borderline.

Once the behavioral symptoms have been identified and throughout the course of treatment the mental health professional assesses the level of impairment caused of each aspect of the disorder. The treatment provider must triage and alleviate the most significant symptoms in relation to impairment. For example, in the case of self-mutilation and suicidal gestures, it is important to understand the backdrop and the function of these behaviors. Self-hatred and depression are treated very differently, than angry attention-seeking behavior, or to alleviate the dissociation the borderline often feels. Self-mutilation is often caused by the need to distract from emotional pain, but sometimes it is just to "feel" something to the woman who feels detached from herself and the world around her. What complicates matters more is that the symptoms, level of impairment, and emotional state are extremely fluid and thus ever-changing.

Psychiatric treatment in isolation is dicey at best. If the psychiatrist chooses to treat depression and anxiety with anti-depressants, he may trigger manic or bipolar symptoms. If he administers mood stabilizers to treat bipolar episodes, the resultant flattened affect could exacerbate dissociative symptoms and result in non-compliance with treatment due to the borderline's "need to feel" intensely. Anti-anxiety medications could easily be misused and may provide a means for the borderline to commit suicide by alcohol and drug overdose. Weight gain associated with atypical antipsychotics is often unacceptable to patients with co-morbid eating disorders. Medication needs to be carefully monitored and adjusted if used at all.

To further complicate matters, all classes of medication commonly used take weeks or months to titrate to effective dosages and need to be gradually decreased for discontinuation. By the time the medication to treat the identified symptoms reaches a therapeutic level, the symptoms that most need treating have likely changed. This often results in complicated "medication cocktails" with

unpredictable side effects, adverse
reactions, and interaction effects.

Psychotherapy can be helpful and is an
important adjunct to any medication
treatment. Most psychiatrists do not treat
patients on a frequent enough basis to
evaluate symptom, effectively triage and
modify the medication regimen. On-going
and frequent communication between the
psychologist, or other skilled mental health
therapist and the psychiatrist is of
paramount importance, with an unstable
borderline. While this is the "gold
standard" or "best practice" the
constraints imposed by managed health
care companies in terms of fee structure
and covered services often prevent health
professionals from devoting the necessary
time to communicate and coordinate
services.

But, does psychotherapy really help? My resounding answer to this question is, "It depends". In fact, in some cases, I would venture to say it is harmful. Remember, borderline personality disorder is characterized by intense and volatile interpersonal relationships. This occurring in the patient-therapist relationship is a given. Therapists must be skilled and emotionally able to manage that relationship without being drawn into the borderline interaction dynamic.

Some modes of psychotherapy have shown great promise. Namely Cognitive-behavioral approaches including Rational-Emotive Behavior Therapy, Cognitive Behavioral Therapy, and Dialectic Behavior Therapy have helped many women. Other modes of therapy including humanistic approaches and psychodynamic approaches have major limitations.

In cognitive-behavior therapy the patient is taught that they can control their behavior and emotions through rational thought. They are trained to identify intense emotional reactions and the irrational or flawed thinking leading to those emotions. Patients are taught to replace the incorrect thinking with more rational and realty based cognitions. Patients are also encouraged to examine and change their self-destructive and aggressive behaviors.

Humanistic-existential approaches focus on unconditional acceptance of the patient. This is often perceived as acceptance of the irrational and yes "crazy" behavior the patient is exhibiting. The patient is inadvertently reinforced for borderline behavior is given positive attention for engaging in self-mutilation, aggressive, and otherwise self-destructive behaviors. In addition, she is given a forum to rehearse her irrational thinking with a highly respected professional, thus making it strongly imbedded within their persona.

Psychoanalysis and other psychodynamic approaches often focus on giving the patent insight into the roots of the disorder. They focus on transference and counter-transference and dig up historical traumatic parent-child interactions. These "insights" without providing the proper tools to maintain rational thinking only serve to increase the irrational thoughts, excessive emotional reactivity, and severe behavioral difficulties.

Most importantly the therapist must be highly intelligent and flexible in his approach. He must never stick to firmly to a treatment plan without carefully assessing the patient each and every time he sees her. Addressing homework and homework compliance is important, but in my opinion manualized treatment such as dialectic behavior therapy has its drawbacks managing the ever and rapidly changing presentation and needs of the patient.

Often patients require short-term hospitalization in order to stabilize and provide for their safety. One should clearly delineate with the patients; the cause and effect of their behaviors and involuntary hospitalization. Suicide attempts must be taken seriously and should be addressed as emergencies even in cases where the line between suicidal gesture and attempt is blurred.

Can women treat women? One might ask if all women are psychotic, is it reasonable to say that woman treating women is akin to the blind, leading the blind? I would not go so far to say yes, but I would suggest some cautionary warnings. First off women mental health providers must be highly insightful into their own mental and emotional state in order to be effective. They must confine their "craziness" to their personal lives. Treating borderline personality disorder is extremely difficult due to the constant emotional manipulation the patient engages in all social interaction. Women, who are by nature more emotionally unstable than men, will likely find this more challenging. In addition to this problem, they can more easily identify with the irrational thinking of the patient and actually encourage some absurd beliefs.

Here is a prime example. A patient of mine described a situation in couples counseling when his wife complained to the female therapist. Her husband being cruel to her for not calling during the day to remind her how much he loved her. My patient explained to the wife and woman therapist that he was very busy at work and was often unable to make phone calls. He further stated that her belief that he didn't love her was not based in reality. He was simply too busy to call. Her perception of his motivation for not calling was incorrect. The therapist berated this man by saying, "Don't you know perception is reality!"

In this case the therapist by siding with the wife, and not allowing for the possibility of misperceiving situations and events allowed the wife's negative self-talk to continue to go unchecked.

Of course, it would be an over-generalization to state that women cannot be effective therapists, but if the therapist is a hugger, kisses you hello, and goodbye, or offers you a lock of her hair this should serve as a red flag, and perhaps it would be best to seek out a male therapist.

As we are putting this work together, we draw on our personal experiences, with patients as well as individuals we have known personally. We struggle with how much of our personal lives to write about here. We also of course want to avoid any identifying information about the individuals discussed here. But at the same time, there are people we have known, and have known well, whose stories are so relevant to this work, that they simply can't be omitted. The following discusses a person I have known very well, via long term relationship. I'm also hesitant to talk about this one person...no hesitant isn't the right word. Afraid is more accurate. Afraid of incurring the wrath of this person, and even fearful of my very life.

That probably sounds like an exaggeration doesn't it? But no, it really isn't. This person exhibits all the traits of the borderline disorder, over a long period of time and to a marked degree. All of the "qualities" of the borderline personality are contained in a small package, that stands around 5'3". The jealous rages, the need for constant attention, the deep down self-loathing, the co-morbid depression and eating disorders. I'm fearful for my life in this situation because my life has been threatened by this individual. Even the language of the threats is familiar. "I'll stab you in the heart!"

That might not sound like a very realistic threat, but in determining the risk level, that is the likelihood that a person is a danger to themselves or others, many factors must be considered. Access to weapons is by far not the least of these. This person was granted access to weapons by the very agency who's sworn responsibility is "to protect and serve". The county police department granted this person a permit to purchase, own, and even carry a handgun. I was even consulted by the issuing police department, but if I had expressed even the slightest reservation about his woman obtaining the permit, I would have been outed as the reason for the permit's denial, and subjected to the rage. I decided I would le the police department make their own decision, independent of my input. But, much to my shock and awe, they granted the permit despite the person admitting to a history of depression, and a history of both psychiatric and psychological treatment for depression and other "Issues". Anyway, when this story hits the presses, I better either be in the federal witness protection program, or at least have a team of ex-special forces body guards.

And where to I begin to you about his person. She is the Queen of the Borderlines. She is the inspiration behind this book. Perhaps I can start with more recent events and work my way backwards. Recently, I was accused of being disrespectful and even being abusive. The disrespect and abuse I was accused of stems from an incident where I was being berated for 35 mins. My crime of disrespect and abuse was that I looked at the clock, to see how long I had to listen and listen in silence as I was repeatedly tong lashed. That's right. My newest offense was merely timing the verbal onslaught. I had timed these before. There were occaisons where my haranguing's lasted for up to two hours. They often happened when I was watching my favorite baseball team, or when I was trying to focus on balancing my check book, or some other necessary but tedious endeavor. My latest scolding was over when I was going to do a household chore. It ended in tears, but they weren't mine. The tearful utterances proclaimed as abusive and deliberately hurtful. The time previous to this I was accused of never appreciating all that is done for me. The cooking, the cleaning, etc. "But I do appreciate it". "No you don't!". This is not unusual at all. I'm told exactly how I feel about something. I'm told I don't care. I'm called controlling. I don't see myself as being controlling at all. In fact, I think this a clear cut case of the pot calling the kettle black. I'm accused of being controlling by a person who wants to know the exact moment I made a decision to to something. Anything. For example, if I stated that I was meeting a few friends for drinks, my accuser would want to know when I was asked, and when I accepted the invitation. And pity me if I held onto this information and did not immediately share it. But I am labeled as controlling. This comes from a person who asks, "Why did you do that?" Why did you put that there? If I were to walk out to retrieve something from my car, I'd be asked, "where did you go?' Answer: "I went to my car". Why? What did you need to get? I f I went to the store, "What store did you go to?' What did you buy? Hmmm. These sound like things a controlling person might say and do? That's what I thought you'd say.

Now these behaviors I just described, annoying as they may be, are not borderline in and of themselves. What is borderline is the reaction when I don't cooperate with the interrogation. I can't say things like "nevermind, it's not important", because that will trigger a rage full of screaming, yelling, cursing, and even threats. Why would I put up with this type of behavior? Well, what choice to I have. Because of my very nature as a heterosexual male, who choses to have relationships with women, that makes me fair game for the rampant mood swings, splitting, rages, and boo-hoo-hooing. Let's not forget, all woman are borderline. So unless I choose to be celibate like a monk in a monastery, or be alone forever, I like the vast majority of my male brethren are faced with the day to day proof of the aphorism "Women, you can't live with them, and you can't live without them". And everywhere you look, you can find many examples in our society of the virtual insanity of women. In art, movies, television, this theme is presented to us time and time again in many different ways.

Personal Reflections and Disclaimers

As I attempt to put the proverbial bow on this this gift to mankind, (and womankind), I feel it important to express the authors' personal beliefs and emotions regarding what has been written here.

Lest anyone call the authors women-haters, misogynists, or male chauvinist pigs, in all honesty, we LOVE women. In fact we ADORE women. We love everything about them. In fact, we obsess about them. We adore the way they look, the way they feel, the way they smell, the way they talk, the way they primp themselves with makeup and hair products, and yes, even the way the act when they behave in true psychotic fashion. We fantasize about these women and at times encourage borderline behavior.

This is a commentary on heterosexual men in general. We feed off of the attention of women; both the positive attention and the negative. They thrill us. Our minds wander to the adoration they provide and the pain they inflict. We are unable to control our impulse to increase the intimacy of our interactions with them. This is a subject for one of our future

projects and will be addressed in more detail at a later date.
Suffice it to say that we worship woman and the psychosis that comes along with them.

However, as previously stated we have reason to fear women. The unpredictability and instability they bring to our lives is often terrifying. Salman Rushdie published the book Satanic Verses. An Iranian mullah issued a Fatwah against him. Essentially, this is a bounty on his head, which now stands at 3.3 million dollars. Mr. Rushdie offended a relatively small but significant segment of the earth's population. We do not take a position on Mr. Rushdie's book, and would never seek to criticize religious beliefs.

I merely, state facts. Many of these facts are commonly held ones that most people including women acknowledge as truth.

The effect of stating these things, and putting ink to paper, in such a candid and sometimes humorous manner is akin to throwing a match into gasoline soaked explosives. We risk offending slightly over fifty percent of the human population. This is the same fifty percent that we have clearly identified as dangerously psychotic.

In borderline lingo, there are trigger words, which can often lead to psychotic reactions. Therapists avoid using these trigger words and advise loved one's of borderline women to do the same. This is a trigger book; a compilation of approximately 30,000 trigger words artistically composed. I and quite aware of what we have done and have no regrets about it. Our goal here is to educate, inform, and hopefully entertain. Another project currently under consideration is more of a practical handbook on managing borderline behavior. This is a huge undertaking that promises to provide relief to all. Have patience, Dear Reader.

So I will end this book with a heartfelt plea to all our beloved female audience. My intention here was not to hurt you, or debase you. If I am guilty of anything, it is exposing your nature with the hope of empowering you to grow and find peace and happiness within yourself. It is not a judgment or condemnation. So please, I beg you, do not place a bounty upon my head, try to refrain from spitting in my face, do not break my bones, shoot me, bludgeon me, or stab me in the heart. I respect you all and thank you for being the person you are.

I also want to go a step further and say something that may seem quite cliché'. What is the answer? What is the most powerful healing thing we can do? What can possibly prevent this disorder from developing in the first place? The best answer I have to that is not scientific, or clinical, yet I truly believe it. The answer is LOVE! Yes, with all my training and expertise, and years of practice, this is what it all boils down to? Yes, I believe so. I believe that at the heart of this disorder is a fundamental breakdown in love. In feeling unloved by a parent, or by being abused by an uncle (a perversion of love), the individual develops with a void, within their sense of self. And as I have told many of my patients and others, I don't care how strong we feel our self-esteem is, or feelings of self-love are, if everywhere we went, we received nothing but hostility and hatred, from every, single person we encountered, it would eventually take its toll on our perception of our own self-worth. We develop feelings of our self-worth initially from external sources, from our parents, our family, our first friendships, our teachers, etc. This forms the basis for our sense of self. Do we feel worthy or not? Worthy of being loved and in turn, of giving love. So my final words are the following. Gentlemen (or ladies if you are so inclined), love the women in your life. Accept their frailties and insecurities, and simply love them. Ladies, accept nothing but love in your relationships. Believe that you ARE indeed worthy and deserving of the love of another human being. Recognize when you have it, and if you don't, be aware of when it is offered to you. Do not fear love, or flee from it. Love has the power to truly heal us, and make us whole. We must appreciate and accept the at-times stark differences between the genders. Value each and every opportunity to give and receive love. Adore and treasure the people who love you in your life, because, and tragically so, it is often only when we lose someone we love, until then, are we

able to greatly and fully appreciate that
which we have lost.

References:

Diagnostic and statistical manual of mental disorders: DSM-5.
(2013). Washington, D.C.: American Psychiatric Association.

Fatal attraction: [Motion picture]. (1987). United States:
Paramount Pictures.

Kessler RC, McGonagle KA, Zhao S, Nelson CB, Hughes M,
Eshleman S, et al. Lifetime and 12- month prevalence of DSM-
III-R psychiatric disorders in the United States. Results from
the National Comorbidity Survey. Arch Gen Psychiatry
1994;51(1):8-19.

Kessler RC. Epidemiology of psychiatric comorbidity. In:
Tsuang MT, Tohan M, Zahner GEP, eds. Textbook in Psychiatric
Epidemiology. New York, NY: John Wiley & Sons Inc., 1995:
179-197. McEwen BS, Alves SE, Bulloch K. Ovarian steroids and
the brain: Implications for cognition and aging. Neurology
1997;48, Suppl 7:S8-S15.

Robins LN, Locke BZ, Regier DA. An overview of psychiatric
disorders in America. In: Robins LN, Regier DA, eds. Psychiatric
Disorders in America: The Epidemiologic Catchment Study.
New York, NY: Free Press, 1991: 328-366.

Star Trek: Amok time [Motion picture]. (1967). Hollywood, CA: Paramount.

Weissman MM, Bland RC, Canino GJ, Faravelli C, Greenwald S, Hwu HG, et al. Cross-national epidemiology of major depression and bipolar disorder. JAMA 1996;276(4):293-9. * Yonkers KA, Ellison JM, Shera DM, et al. Description of antipanic therapy in a prospective longitudinal study. Journal of Clinical Psychopharmacology 1996;16(3):223-32.

www.ingramcontent.com/pod-product-compliance
Lightning Source LLC
Chambersburg PA
CBHW062138280526
45788CB00001B/210